DEVELOPING WORLD CLASS LEADERS

The Ultimate Guide to Leadership Development

Rick Tiemann

Developing World Class Leaders—The Ultimate Guide to Leadership Development

®16PF is a registered trademark of The Institute for Personality and Ability Testing, Inc. (IPAT). IPAT is a subsidiary of Performance Assessment Network, Inc. (PAN).

Copyright in the 16PF Manual, IPAT, PAN. 1801 Woodfield Drive, Savoy, IL 61874, USA. All rights reserved.

For information about this title or to order other books and/or electronic media, contact the publisher:
Richard K. Tiemann
80 East US Highway 6, Valparaiso, IN 46383
www.theeg.com
assessment@theeg.com

978-0-9905349-07 (Paperback)
978-0-9905349-14 (eBook)

Printed in the United States of America
Cover and Interior design: 1106 Design

To Dad, for teaching leadership by example.
To Mom, for the continuous faith and support.

Contents

What They're Saying

"When I took over the Asian Operations in Suzhou, China, I soon recognized I needed to build a stronger management team. I knew with Rick's background in international business, he would be the logical choice to help make this happen. Rick's concepts in management and leadership development, and his understanding of the cultural differences in play within an international organization, have proven valuable whenever I need to make decisions that have a major impact on my organization."
—**John Jofre**, President, Asia Synventive Molding Solutions

"Rick has been in my corner now for almost a decade. I consider him to be a key element in my resource arsenal. Beyond his phenomenal depth of understanding of the psychological tools and instruments, it is his ability to put things into the business context that makes him such a valuable go-to resource to me.

Because of his wide and deep business experience and his work with such a wide range of organizations he simply gets it! He grasps the subtleties of the issues I deal with and we can cut to the chase when exploring issues.

For me, *Developing World Class Leaders* is a structured look at the real issues in leadership development in the corporate world that most of us stumble over. It is not complex stuff but, rather, it is disciplined work inside some basic truths and constructs. I'd liken Rick to a "Leadership Development Physicist," who has seen and knows natural law. Like gravity, when you don't do X you don't get Y. He has done a solid job of giving us a path to success to leadership development with this work."

—**Tom Brown,** Director of Talent Management, Printpack, Inc.

"Rick Tiemann has made a career of looking into the very soul of people. When his mastery of the tools of assessment are coupled with a lifetime of C-level leadership experience, he gives a whole new foundation to the saying, "hire slow, fire fast."

—**Stewart McMillan,** President, Task Force Tips

"Rick brings an experienced and objective perspective to strategy and leadership development. He asks the tough questions that you can't or don't always want to ask yourself. He then helps develop answers that can bring significant change and a sense of being in better control of the organization's future."

—**Russ Holmer,** President, Haumiller Engineering

From the Author

I was inspired to write this book after people attending my workshops called *The Process of Leadership* said that none of their organizations had an in-depth leadership development program covering the depth of information I had presented. The attendees came because they wanted to learn how to develop such a leadership program in their organization. The content I used in my workshops became the chapters of this book.

My appreciation for leadership development began during my four years at Fishburne Military School, an institution that focuses on preparing young men to lead. The very foundation of its principles, programs, and curriculum emulates a successful leadership development program. Great men who were my mentors and instructors helped me understand the responsibilities of a leadership position. Colonel E. B. Young, Major Norton, Major Pitman, Captain Cross, Captain "Shep" Shepard, and Captain Mullin helped shape and prepare me for my future. In my senior year I became the battalion commander of the cadet corps and that experience exposed me to the challenges of leadership and the lessons of life. It was an amazing learning experience, and I thank all of the aforementioned individuals for helping me.

Other leaders from my parents to instructors to clients have provided invaluable guidance and shaped my career and my work. I thank all of you because I could have never accomplished this feat on my own. My goal was to write a "how-to" book that outlines a comprehensive program dedicated to helping companies develop a World Class Leadership Development Program. I hope you find it hits the mark.

Regards,
Rick Tiemann, President
The Executive Group
www.theeg.com

Introduction
Developing World Class Leaders
The Ultimate Guide to Leadership Development

Welcome! In the following chapters I will provide a comprehensive approach on how to develop world class leaders. This method is a fully integrated development program that entails every component that is necessary to build a world class leadership development program. This program is a distillation of my consulting work of twenty-five years and more than forty years of business experience.

Throughout my career in business and, more specifically, as a consultant, I have found that relatively few companies have an in-depth leadership development program; and even the ones that do rarely fully utilize it or continue to use it over the long haul. In chapter 2, I will review the many reasons why this happens and why they often fail to achieve the desired outcome.

Having worked closely with well over 200 companies over these last twenty-five years, I've identified several essential components required to develop a world class leadership development program. This book will examine these factors, from setting the programs up to making adjustments according to the needs of your particular company. Your company may already have some of these elements in place but, in reality, I have discovered that few companies have a cohesive leadership development program. Instead, I see companies take shortcuts that impact the efficiency of the entire program. The problem is very few companies utilize all of the components together in a comprehensive leadership development program. As you learn about each of the elements, you'll begin to understand why they are all essential to the success of the program. You can't simply pick and choose the ones you like or want to use and ignore the others.

By having a complete development program and using it over time, you will see a dramatic improvement in the performance of your business leaders and, ultimately, in your business results. When you have fully developed your employees in the appropriate roles, you should see exponential business results, because the leaders in those roles will have the needed technical skills, the right job competencies, and the proper behaviors to lead effectively. As we begin to explore the world of developing successful leaders, I would like to share with you a statement that has stuck with me for years:

"Upon promotion into management, one becomes mystically endowed, with all the traits necessary to hire and create a team that gets the job done."

Even though this anonymous statement is obviously tongue-in-cheek, it is relevant to today's business world and the contents of this book. Before you get into the "meat" of the book, here are two important questions worth asking:

Why is it that some leaders are more successful than others?

Why is the "Peter Principle" alive and well today?

If you are not familiar with the Peter Principle it will be explained in detail in chapter 2. This book will not only address and answer these questions, it will also address why most leadership programs are destined to fail and what you can to do to prevent such failure within your organization. Throughout my years of consulting I have come to believe that a company's success is largely predicated on the success and skills of its management team.

Assuming this statement is true, then why don't companies, including yours, spend more time and effort developing a world class leadership development program to advance their leaders? After all, if the leaders of today, and especially the leaders of tomorrow, will make or break your organization, why wouldn't you invest in a process and system for developing them and implement it to its fullest? Imagine what would happen if a manufacturing company did not conduct preventive maintenance on their equipment. The same principles apply to people. Investing in human capital and then not developing them to their full potential is no different than investing in the best equipment and then not maintaining it. Doing anything less means your bottom line results will always be disappointing.

It is important to emphasize that the elements outlined in this book require each one to be part of an ongoing process; each component should not be treated as a separate event. Too often portions or sections of the program are picked out of the process because there is an issue that needs to be addressed with one executive and a quick fix is used to address a particular situation. For example, it is not uncommon to put an executive who is struggling or in crisis through a 360-Degree Assessment. Typically the organization does not want to single him or her out so all the executives go through the 360 process. Unfortunately the 360 rarely gets significant traction, and the intended effort goes nowhere, because the troubled executive gets lost in the process. As a result, the executive never really sees this assessment as an intervention or understands that he or she has a problem because the person's issues disappear as part of a larger initiative. The unfortunate outcome is the rest of the organization sees this as just another futile effort or the flavor of the month. I will explain more about why most 360 assessments never bring about the needed changes and what to do about it in chapter 5, "Creating an Internal Feedback Loop."

The subsequent chapters will get into the details behind why each component is necessary to build a successful program. As in any program there is usually a process or some type of system, strategy, or outline that needs to be followed. This is no different than a company that maintains its manufacturing process by following ISO standards to help keep the corporation in compliance and on track. In my work I have identified the key components which I have come to find are necessary to build a successful leadership development program. The following chapters will explain in detail the aspects of each area.

Developing World Class Leaders

- A well-defined business strategy
- A well-defined corporate culture that supports leadership development
- A leadership competency model that supports the strategic intent
- Assessments that evaluate the depth of talent within the organization
- Honest and direct feedback from multiple perspectives
- Accountability reinforced top down, not by HR alone
- Ongoing, continuous personal and professional development
- An established leadership pipeline
- A viable succession plan

I have been around corporate America in many roles for more than four decades. For ten years in the 1970s, I owned my own businesses. For another ten-year period in the 1980s, I was director of sales and marketing, vice president of sales, and Asian business development manager. At one point in my career, I was president of a $75-million-dollar company in the fire and security industry. Since 1991, when I started The Executive Group, I have been consulting with businesses in the areas of talent management, organizational development, and business development. One of the main focuses has been on leadership selection, development, and executive coaching. The reason for writing this book and telling you about my background is that throughout my extensive years of experience, I have yet to find an organization fully committed to the depth of developing a World Class Leadership Program as it is outlined here. The reasons for this are varied and many, and I will provide explanations as to why leadership programs fail in chapter 2. The chapters that follow will guide you through the steps necessary to assure a successful outcome.

Many times senior leadership talks about investing in their leaders and creating development plans but make little if any commitment to the process of doing so, let alone focus on their own personal development. Rarely do they give priority to making sure they create development plans for themselves.

*"Everyone thinks of changing the world,
but no one thinks of changing himself."*
—Leo Tolstoy, Russian novelist

Tolstoy said it best when it comes to professional development. When I ask individuals how they see their strengths and weaknesses they always talk about everything except themselves personally. I have experienced this numerous times over the years where leadership does not "walk the talk." One organization I worked with did nothing to challenge its senior leaders to develop themselves. Several members of the leadership team were visibly weak yet nothing was done to address their deficiencies. Perhaps you have heard the term "sacred cow." Well, it existed within this organization, and it exists in corporate America. It cripples the organization in many ways and holds them back from reaching their full potential.

In working with this organization, I discussed conducting a 360-degree feedback process on the key leaders for their development. However, management decided it was not something they wanted to do, justifying their decision by saying it was not something they wanted to IMPOSE on senior leaders. Yet they claimed they wanted to create a leadership development program. It is impossible to develop top-notch leaders without a dynamic development program in place to hold your leaders accountable to an established set of standards. Not wanting to impose a 360 program says a lot about a company's culture. Leadership development is not something you IMPOSE on your leaders. It is something you should EXPECT from your leaders. This speaks volumes about a company's culture.

In consulting with senior members from the leadership team of another organization, the discussion turned to leadership within the organization and one of the more senior executives commented, "I believe we have a good learning organization." I asked why they thought that and asked if they had read Peter Senge's book, *The Fifth Discipline* on building a learning organization. The reply came back, "Oh, I don't read those kinds of books; I don't have time for them." This is yet another example of being able to gauge the level of commitment by what leadership says. Listening closely to what members of the leadership team discuss reveals a great deal about the culture of the organization and how it feels about leadership development.

It is my hope that this book will help influence the thought process of those at the top regarding what it takes to develop not only their leaders but themselves. These are some of the significant points I will address throughout this book:

- The fundamental components of a successful leadership program

- Why most leadership programs don't produce desired results

- Why and how leaders stagnate

- How leadership impacts strategic intent

- How great leadership is related to emotional intelligence

- The significance of critical thinking skills on leadership

- How behavior impacts leadership

- Creating developmental initiatives and exercises

The content in this book will help you address each of these items and more. As you read through this book, at the end of each chapter, ask yourself the following:

"On a scale of 1 to 5, with 5 being the highest, how would you rate your leadership team, and how would you rate your leadership program and its results against the chapter you just read?"

If you are interested in finding out how your leadership program rates, take our leadership survey at www.leader shipculturesurveyonline.com to find out how your program stacks up.

You owe it to the people of your organization and the leaders of your organization to develop a world class leadership development program. This will, in turn, set the stage to develop a world class organization with world class leaders.

By reading this book you have taken the first step, but this is only the beginning. You need to execute each of the components outlined here to the fullest and not cut corners. I wish you the best in your quest to develop a strong, sustaining world class leadership development program. I hope you find the contents and the program outlined in this book beneficial in supporting your leadership initiatives.

1

Building the Case for Leadership Development

In order for you to understand how essential it is to have the right leadership development program in your organization, it's useful to see what happens when a high-level executive has a very dramatic fall from grace. Here are the stories of three very prominent individuals who once sat in the executive chair of three renowned companies. They all were leaders at some of the most prestigious companies in the world but, after very brief tenures, they were asked to resign by the very board of directors that had promoted them.

In each case, the impact their departure had on the company was as devastating as it was to their own careers. As you read their stories, consider the following questions:

- How could leaders of this magnitude, at these levels and in these kinds of companies, fail so miserably?

- How could this happen given their background and experience?

- How was it that the board of directors was unaware of their shortcomings?

- How could the board of directors have done a better job of determining whether the executives were fit for the top spot?

- Was the leadership development and succession plan somehow flawed?

- Are these outcomes proof that the Peter Principle really exists?

- What can be learned by studying their downfalls?

Before I get into their stories, here are some statistics worth noting. While this information is slightly dated it still has merit when it comes to showing the need for evaluating a leader's skills and abilities before we hire or promote them, regardless of how much we think we know them. At the 1,000 largest American companies (by revenue) in 2008, eighty new CEOs were appointed, but only forty-four of them (55 percent) were promoted from within. What do you think this statistic says about leadership, the leadership programs, and the succession planning necessary to develop successful leaders? Is it reasonable to say there is a breakdown in the system when 45 percent of CEOs are hired from outside a company? The statistics support the notion that creating a world class leadership development program is required in order to create a robust pipeline and create a strong succession plan. As you read through these examples, consider how three very successful, prominent, and apparently capable individuals self-destruct in just a few short years. How did their actions grow so flagrant or harmful that they were asked to resign by the very boards who selected them?

■ Story #1 Doug Ivester—Coca-Cola

This headline was for an article in *FORTUNE Magazine* (January 10, 2000), "What Really Happened at Coke"[1]

Doug Ivester was promoted to CEO of Coca-Cola by the Board of Directors and, in just a few short years, he was asked to resign by the very board who was responsible for promoting him. What did they miss? Where did they go wrong? This is a classic example of promoting the apparent next in line and assuming that past performance would predict future performance. I encourage you to read the whole article about what led to his downfall at the age of fifty-two, after only a little more than two years on the job.

Loyalty and longevity, coupled with company knowledge and experience, is often valued over real capability. In this case Doug Ivester, the longtime CFO and Roberto Goizueta's

---

[1] Betsy Morris and Patricia Sellers, "What Really Happened at Coke," *Fortune*, Jan. 10, 2000. Retrieved from http://fortune.com/2012/11/21/what-really-happened-at-coke/ on Nov. 27, 2015.

second in command, was rewarded for his financial savvy and years of loyalty and was promoted to the top spot after Goizueta's death. The difficulties that caused his failure seem like things that any CEO at this level should be able to master. A serious slide in the company's share price, some bad public-relations moves, and poor handling of a product contamination scare in Europe showed just a few of the gaps in his ability and caused his downfall. The real question and, perhaps, even the bigger issue is why there was not enough attention paid to his current skills and abilities and how they would apply to the broader role. When any board or any organization wrongly assumes that an individual has all the characteristics necessary to succeed at the next level, and fails to truly evaluate an individual's potential, you are bound to have a similar result.

■ Story #2 Jill Barad–Mattel

An article in *The Wall Street Journal* on February 4, 2000, featured the following headline: "Jill Barad Resigns as Mattel CEO as Toymaker's Results Suffer."

The article then stated, "Jill Barad, one of the highest profile women in corporate America, resigned as chairman and chief executive of Mattel, Inc., ending a turbulent three-year tenure marked by a disastrous acquisition and a stream of earnings disappointments."[2]

---

[2] Lisa Bannon and Joan S. Lublin, "Jill Barad Resigns as Mattel CEO as Toymaker's Results Suffer," *The Wall Street Journal*, Feb. 4, 2000. Retrieved from http://www.wsj.com/articles/SB949609433757217239 on Nov. 27, 2015.

Much like the example of Doug Ivester, Jill Barad's winning track record in marketing catapulted her into the top job at Mattel. Again, similar to the example of Coca-Cola's CEO, her marketing background didn't give her insight into the financial and strategic aspects of running a large corporation. To her credit she had grown Mattel's Barbie brand nearly tenfold in less than a decade and, much like Ivester, Mattel rewarded her prior successes without further analysis about her readiness to handle the top spot. What contributed to her downfall was a controlling management style, a lack of experience in finance and strategy, as well as the mishandling of Wall Street. You would think that a highly capable and qualified CEO would be able to master these competencies but, in her case, these skills were severely lacking.

Again we must address the notion that if more due diligence about her skills and abilities was done prior to her promotion, could an early intervention have exposed these limitations and provided an opportunity for her to develop these skills and helped her keep her career on track? A well-constructed leadership assessment program might have revealed potential weaknesses and the company could have either prepared her for the assignment or decided early on that she wasn't ready for a role of this magnitude. Yet the board wrongly assumed Barad was ready and suffered the consequences for a lack of due diligence. This again supports the need for a robust leadership development program that includes a robust leadership assessment process.

■ Story #3 Jeffrey Skilling—Enron

On June 21, 2013, Jeffrey Skilling made the news with the downfall of Enron. He was touted as having a reputation as a smart, extremely competitive businessman with a penchant for risk-taking qualities that led to his early success and facilitated his rise to the executive suite. These attributes became counterproductive, however, when Skilling's unconscious biases began to shape Enron's culture. Creative risk-taking and fierce internal competition coupled with huge incentives led to not only stretching, but circumventing and breaking legal and ethical boundaries to bolster the company's short-term performance. How can such a bright, highly successful individual not only destroy his own career but the career of others—let alone an entire company? When titles and egos override sound business values and ethics the outcomes are usually counterproductive or worse.

In Skilling's case he was convicted on nineteen counts, including twelve counts of securities fraud and one count of insider trading. Skilling's offenses added up to thirty-six points under the federal sentencing guidelines, which would have resulted in a sentence of 188 to 235 months, or fifteen to nineteen years. But the trial judge added a four-point "enhancement" because Skilling allegedly jeopardized the safety and soundness of a financial institution, namely the employee retirement plans. That four-point enhancement meant Skilling could be sentenced to far more time, 292 to 365 months or twenty-four to thirty years. The result was one of the harshest sentences ever handed down for a white-collar crime. Where was the board? How was it that no one saw this coming? How was Skilling allowed to lead in such a fashion and be so reckless?

These are certainly the stories that make headlines. More importantly, these are the stories that support the need for a well-designed leadership development program. Perhaps such a program might have created a different outcome for these executives. At the very least it supports the notion that there is a need to assess the capabilities of your leaders no matter what their previous track record looks like.

▪ Leadership Lessons

Ivester, Barad, and Skilling failed. Although each of them was accomplished in at least one area of management, we can safely conclude none had mastered more significant competencies such as public relations, designing and managing acquisitions, and building trust among Wall Street insiders. While these specific experiences are significant and suggest that leadership development still has a long way to go, even at large and prominent companies in America, there are many other similar cases and there are probably even bigger concerns lurking. The problem is not just that the shoes of the departed are too big; it's that succession planning, as traditionally conceived and executed, is often too narrow and limited to uncover and correct skill gaps that can derail even the most promising young executives, not to mention experienced executives such as the ones mentioned here.

If nearly half of all CEOs come from outside an organization, it seems apparent that there is an issue. The shortcomings of the leadership system seem even more insidious when promoted executives fail within a short period of time after being promoted. And, they don't just fall short and then quietly depart. Their downfalls are so repugnant that their employers' boards of directors asked them to leave.

When this kind of scenario does happen we really need to step back and ask some key questions. Was there no leadership development program in place? Was there no assessment process in place? Was the program that was in place of poor quality? Did the company circumvent the process and not take the proper steps to assure the right choices were being made? Exploring this further we could ask if the reasons are due to the fact that companies have not done effective succession planning or don't have qualified talent developed well enough to take on new roles at higher levels. It could suggest a lack of capable individuals who are ready to step up and take over key roles to fill a pipeline. Perhaps, there is no system for interviews and detailed evaluation and assessment to determine gaps in employee skills. In the aforementioned cases, it is fair to assume that the board assumed the people were capable enough and the organization felt it knew them well enough but, by the results, it is fair to say they missed the mark. It is not enough to state the obvious; we must understand what was missed and make sure we don't make the same mistake.

These examples merely scratch the surface of failed executives. They speak to a glaring lack of effective leadership programs and overall development of leaders. And while there are executives such as these at this level who fail and make big headlines, undoubtedly there are unqualified people filling key roles in almost every organization today that are less than effective in their current roles. To help see where there is a breakdown in the process, I will provide some case studies in chapter 12 that will explore this topic in depth to show how and why these failures happen. *Developing World Class Leaders* is a comprehensive program designed to offer solutions that will enhance your leadership program and put it on the right path.

■ Further Examples

Just when I thought I had finished this chapter, another glaring example of CEO misbehavior made the headlines. CEO Jeff Smisek, along with two executives at United Airlines, resigned, apparently because of a federal government investigation related to Smisek trading favors with the head of the Port Authority of New York and New Jersey. The list of ousted or embattled CEOs over just the last few years is very long: Dov Charney, founder of American Apparel; Lululemon Athletica founder Dennis Wilson; Abercrombie and Fitch's chief executive Michael Jeffries;

and Restoration Hardware's chairman Gary Friedman are just a few of the examples of failed leaders.

In Closing

How many leaders and even key people in significant positions in your organization are in trouble right now? Can they be helped? How long will you let them continue before you acknowledge that something must change? Ask and answer this vital question: "Can our organization afford NOT to have a world class leadership development program in place?" The answer is obvious. You can't! Therefore, you must start to develop a world class leadership development program and commit to keeping it in place. The following chapters will help you understand what to do and how to go about it but, more importantly, why such a development program is necessary.

2

Why Leadership Development Programs Fail!

In the last chapter, I presented several examples of failed executives that reveal some harsh realities about what it takes to succeed, especially for people in the most senior roles. Upper-level managers and others at the top of organizations face an incredible number of challenges from competitive battles, legal concerns, economy uncertainty, human resource issues, and more. Even the most seasoned executives who have years of experience don't always have what it takes to succeed, particularly during times of catastrophic crises. Even in the greatest of companies in the world, the Peter Principle plays out again and again.

The "Peter Principle" is a concept in management theory first observed by Dr. Laurence Peter. When determining candidates for upper-level positions, Dr. Peter's theory suggests that a candidate's performance in his or her current role, rather than the abilities relevant to the intended role, determines the selection of the candidate for the new position. Thus, employees only stop being promoted once they can no longer perform effectively, and managers rise to the level of their incompetence. Dr. Peter noted the managers' incompetence may be a result of the skills required for the new role being different rather than being more difficult; by way of example, an excellent engineer may find that he isn't an effective manager because he lacks the interpersonal skills required to effectively lead a team. What really stands out in the business world is that the Peter Principle is not only reserved for those who occupy the top spot. The Peter Principle, by its very nature, plays out at every level in every organization. But while Dr. Peter speaks to those skills being different rather than more difficult, which I agree, the dynamics of the examples I have provided support the fact of them being more difficult. Therefore, the leadership assessment component takes on special meaning and relevance.

There are many reasons why people fail in their roles and many of the reasons have to do with not having received specific leadership development training. There are often training programs for specific task-related skills, such as engineering, accounting, or design. But, too often, managers are not taught how to be more effective leaders. It is assumed that if you're successful at accomplishing specific tasks or reaching financial targets, you will naturally be a great leader. But that's not the case. There needs to be a way to identify these potential concerns ahead of time, identify the gaps, and then prepare leaders for their challenges ahead.

Just as important is having a process that helps identify the right leader for a particular role rather than assuming an individual has all the traits necessary to succeed just because he or she was successful in a lessor or different role. There are many reasons why leadership development programs fail to succeed and deliver successful outcomes. In this chapter I will share my views about why leadership development programs fail to deliver favorable results. I will also give you examples of the most common mistakes and where your organization may be falling short.

In almost every case, it's not just one thing that impacts poor results but a culmination of many factors that cause leadership development programs to fall short. The following are twelve scenarios to consider that may be undermining your program. In all likelihood, a combination of these dynamics is involved, but in some cases it is the last item listed. You may be tempted to just skip through and see what the last item is, but I encourage you to review each point. Examine each of the twelve points and determine for yourself which ones are applicable in your organization.

Twelve Reasons Why Leadership Programs Fail

1. Leadership Development Is Not a Strategic Corporate Initiative

Unfortunately, leadership development rarely exists as a strategic corporate initiative, which means there is almost never a robust leadership development program. This initiative is increasingly more critical considering today's competitive landscape where the talent pool is dwindling and the depth of qualified candidates is low, coupled with the fact that most highly driven people want to be on the fast track.

Financially speaking, there is not a line item on a financial statement that measures leadership or leadership development. Maybe if there were one, more attention might be paid to it. Research and development (R&D) is a line item and is a prerequisite in many companies like manufacturing and software development. R&D is necessary because a company must always be developing new products. So why isn't there a category and line item for developing leaders?

The problem lies in the fact that management often does not OWN leadership development. This is because it is typically housed under human resources and in turn becomes an HR function. I believe that, generally speaking, management does not support leadership development to the degree and extent it should. Talking about it or speaking to it is far different than supporting it and insisting on a world class leadership development program. Management doesn't initiate a program for employees, nor do they push *themselves* to develop new skills, competencies, and behaviors. It's quite typical for the leaders of an organization to expect and want the managers of the organization to go through some type of development, but they never make the commitment to go through the process or fully develop themselves.

Typically the old adage, "What's good for the goose is good for the gander," does not apply to the world of leadership development. Instead the old mind-set of "Do as I say, not as I do" applies.

2. There Is Not a Corporate Culture That Supports Building a Learning Organization

This is related to the first reason regarding leadership as a strategic corporate initiative. To have a culture built around a learning organization suggests the organization expects its employees to develop themselves, which goes hand in hand with having an in-depth leadership development program. In order to build a learning organization, it's important to understand that the corporate culture of the organization must endorse it and support it. Supporting a learning organization has as much to do with the success of a leadership development program as it does with having an effective process, procedure, system, and program in place to develop successful leaders.

From emerging leaders to senior leaders, building an organizational culture of leadership development and continuous learning is challenging. It must be backed up with a robust development program in place to help the organization's leadership initiative succeed and then have a culture that demands it. The mind-set of developing a learning organization is as important as the leadership development process itself. They are dependent on each other, and you can't have one without the other.

3. There Is No Formal Structure, Program, or Process in Place to Follow

An effective leadership program is only as good as the structure and program that is in place. Any building needs a firm foundation to support the structure. More often than not, when you examine an organization's leadership program you'll see there are pieces but not all the parts. Many programs take on a Band-Aid approach because the companies either don't know what is entailed in maintaining a full program, don't have a sufficient budget to fully support it, or don't understand the value of having a complete program. Often an organization knows that it needs to develop its leaders so the organization does something rather than nothing. Consequently, it short circuits the leadership process and, in exchange, shortchanges the leaders' ability to develop themselves. To use a very common analogy, if you skimp on the ingredients when baking a cake, the cake won't rise. Likewise, if you shortchange the process in your leadership development program it's likely to flop as well.

4. Untrained and Inexperienced People Are Put in Place to Oversee or Develop a Program

This tactic is a problem since an inexperienced person or someone who is untrained in overseeing a robust leadership development process will be at a disadvantage. The person may use more trial and error methods as he or she tries to figure out how to build something from scratch.

In addition, the individual is not likely to ever gain the respect within the organization because colleagues will soon realize the inexperienced person doesn't know what to do. If an organization does not have a true organizational development (OD) person in place, it needs to find an outside vendor with that expertise to advise and direct its needs. Without this approach, a company can flounder and will find out later that this is largely the reason the program isn't successful.

5. Limited Staffing Is Allocated to Support the Program and the Process

Typically, there aren't enough people allocated to develop an effective leadership program. Allocation of time, money, and resources are often less than realistic and usually understated, but understaffing will limit the effectiveness of your program. The size and complexity of the organization will determine the staff ratio necessary to implement an effective program. Common sense dictates here as there is no ratio that I am aware of about the necessary number of staff, but it is obviously based on the number of employees. You can't have just one person dedicated to this task in a company with 800 to 1,000 employees, no matter how experienced they are. I have witnessed this scenario and know of its existence and seen the challenges it brings.

6. The Program Is Not Properly Funded

Often, organizations do not commit to enough funding to support a leadership program and wind up falling short in developing and administering a complete leadership program. A budget shortfall in this area means you'll have to omit some aspects of the program that may well be critical to the organization's success. I am still surprised that companies willingly have large advertising or R&D budgets rather than allocating funds to developing their leaders and grooming and growing the talent within the organization.

A strong leadership program helps develop the leadership pipeline and creates an effective succession planning process. One organization I spoke with said it couldn't stress leadership development because its industry operated on low margins and didn't have the budget. This organization had fifty restaurant locations. In the restaurant industry, there is a real problem known as "shrink." This is when food walks out the back door, or liquor is overpoured or free drinks are given to friends. The list goes on, but it is a REAL concern for every restaurant in the world, not just theirs. Okay, so there are low margins, but there are reasons for those low margins. However, what is the cost of having an ineffective general manager at just one restaurant, let alone half of them? The company overlooks that problem and uses the fact that they operate with tight margins as an excuse for not spending the money to establish a leadership program that develops their managers. Is this really good business? What if half the managers of those fifty restaurants are poor managers? What is the cost of mediocrity? What is the cost of not having a world class leadership development program in place?

7. Leadership Development Is Sporadic and Lacks Consistency

Typically, there is no consistency in a leadership development program for many reasons. There are budgetary constraints or priority projects that take precedence. I have even witnessed a new CFO trying to cut costs by slashing the leadership development program. Leadership development will fail if it is associated with *The Idea of the Month*. Then six to twelve months later, another leadership program or another leadership initiative is instituted, and people say, "Well, it didn't hold last time; let's just wait. It'll fall by the wayside again." You can't expect your people to be serious about development if there are no expectations and no one is looking to challenge them, let alone support them.

8. There Is Minimal Accountability or Lack of Follow-up

There is often a lack of accountability. If your leadership development initiative has no one holding individuals accountable for their development, nothing is likely to happen.

There needs to be a follow-up process to ensure individuals are actually sticking to a detailed and approved personal and professional development plan. More often than not, the review process is never created, let alone instituted. Let's take the typical 360. Once it is completed, the odds are extremely high the executives will never do another one. Why? Because going through a 360 was part of their key performance indicators (KPI). It was merely something to be checked off a to-do list. Unfortunately, it was not part of a process to improve their skills; it was merely part of a requirement to complete a 360. There is no follow-up with managers or colleagues to evaluate the results. There is a huge disconnect in this approach. If you live by the honor system, that's great, but it's not a very sustainable way to achieve success. Unless the executive is a self-directed learner, the process is not going to optimize any significant results.

To illustrate this point, here's an example. I was asked to create individual leadership development plans for the thirteen senior managers in the US division of a $4 billion international company. Upon reviewing the 360 results with one of the individuals, the executive looked at me and said, "It's interesting; many of the things that showed up in my last 360 showed up on this one." Interesting to say the least! This happens all too often. The 360 process will be reviewed in more detail in chapter 5, "Creating an Internal Feedback Loop," where I will address the pros and cons in further detail.

9. The Belief That Teaching Managers How to Coach Is a Solution

First let me say that I am a huge proponent of teaching managers how to coach and believe it is an essential competency for every manager to develop. Some people are better at coaching, but you should recognize that coaching is a specialized skill set and an expert profession, which is why there are executive coaches. Teaching managers the process and methodology of coaching is necessary but not practical when in-depth coaching is needed. Chapter 9 is devoted to coaching and explores this strategy in detail.

10. There Is No Assessment Process in Place or, If There Is, It's Usually a Very Weak One

This is a very difficult area because the world of assessments is extremely complex and vast. Everyone is an expert on assessments and everyone selling assessments touts their program as the end all be all. However, just because someone is certified in using an assessment doesn't mean he or she is an expert. There are so many assessments on the market that it can be daunting to determine which ones have value and which ones don't. Imagine that you need to measure something. You could guess or use a yardstick. You could also use a tape measure, a ruler, or even a micrometer. Obviously the micrometer will give you more of an exact reading and greater accuracy, but if you really want to drill down for accuracy, you need to use a laser.

The same is true in the world of assessments. Some are very simple measures of behavior and some are very sophisticated. Most do not measure behavior at a deep enough level to get at the true behaviors of an individual. Many are not reliable enough to have predictive value, which is a difficult concept for the people using them. Chapter 6, "Exploring the World of Assessments," focuses on this subject in more detail. The need for a well-constructed assessment program is an extremely critical component in assessing your leaders and cannot be taken lightly.

11. The Organization Is Not in It for the Long Haul

Leadership development requires an ongoing, sustainable, year-after-year focus, not something done on an as needed or periodic basis. The entire organization must understand the value and significance of having an ongoing world class leadership development program. Any organization that treats any part of the program as a sporadic event is likely to fail.

The problem is a lack of understanding of what goes into a well-designed leadership development program. To be in it for the long haul, organizations must take into consideration how much it will take to fund it annually, what components are required to have a process that is sustainable, and what resources are needed to make it work. I am often asked, "How long it will take?" My answer is, "As long as the organization is in existence, because the quality of leadership is always needed and true development is a lifelong endeavor."

12. The President/CEO Does Not Own It or Treats It Half-heartedly

I have saved the best for last because this is the *most important piece* in the whole process. While I have identified many reasons why leadership programs fail to achieve success, this is the Number One reason why they fail. Everything starts at the top and is reinforced from the top. If the program is seen as merely an HR initiative, and nobody takes it seriously, guess what happens? Mr. President or CEO, if are you committed to the quality and integrity of your company, it is crucial to have a world class leadership development program. To adopt this as a strategic corporate initiative is imperative!

In Closing

You can build a case for every one of the twelve points listed here. If you take the time to evaluate your organization, you'll probably see some of the reasons why your program hasn't worked well. Any one of these items can cause a leadership development program to fail. Lacking in two areas greatly reduces your odds, but having three or more problematic areas reduces your chances drastically of having a successful program. Making a commitment to develop a world class leadership development program as a strategic corporate initiative will lead to dramatic improvements in productivity, morale, retention, and succession planning. If you can accomplish this, everything you do in this area will impact your bottom line exponentially.

To find out how your leadership program stacks up,
I invite you to take our leadership survey at
www.leadershipculturesurveyonline.com.

3

Linking Leadership with Strategic Intent

Creating a world class leadership development program requires your organization to link its leadership development with its strategic intent. This means the leaders of your organization must be in sync with the strategy of the organization and recognize whether or not they are executing the mission and living up to the mission and values of the organization. This seems obvious but, as you will come to understand, it is not always a truism. This really is the basis for a successful business but, as you will come to learn, oftentimes leaders can become disengaged, wind up going in the wrong direction, and make poor decisions. All you have to do is go back and review the previous chapter about fallen leaders. What was it they lacked that caused their downfall? When the business leaders understand and execute the vision and the mission of the business, the odds of success increase exponentially, not only for themselves but for the organization as well. Jim Collins, author of the well-known book, *Good to Great*, had to write a new book after his first one because Circuit City, one of his prime examples, went under after he had touted it in the book.

The only way to successfully link leadership with strategic intent is for a company to have two things in place. First, the firm must have a sound business strategy and business model in place. I would wager that every company president believes he or she does. I would also wager that Circuit City thought it had a sound business plan in place as well. Jim Collins certainly thought the company did. So why did Circuit City go bust? The article in *Time* magazine on Tuesday, Nov 18, 2008, by Anita Hamilton, "Why Circuit City Busted, While Best Buy Boomed," spells it out. This book is not about why businesses fail, it's about why leadership development programs fail. But if the business has a flawed business model, the rest is history, as in the case of Circuit City. This is why I say a key success factor in a strong leadership development program is a company's strategic intent. Leadership development programs CAN ONLY produce the desired results if a clear vision with a compelling message has been articulated from the top of the organization so that the leaders know what to do day in and day out. When this happens the values, mission, and strategies of the company will provide the context for the necessary behaviors and the specific competencies the leaders need to develop at every level. Perhaps if these principles were in place at Circuit City, it might still be around.

If leaders cannot see and understand the vision and remember the company's mission, they will not integrate it into their daily decision making. This is a very simple concept and a key to successful leadership integration that, for some reason, rarely takes place. Linking leadership with strategic intent requires that the leaders of the organization must align their thinking, skill sets, and competencies with the strategic intent of the organization. If they are not aligned, the leaders' performances are likely to fall short by making poor decisions and even perhaps derail themselves or the business because they will not make consistent choices about what is right and wrong as it relates to business outcomes. Just look at the outcome of Jeffrey Skilling's decisions. Doing this requires the establishment of a set of leadership competencies that I will discuss in the next chapter.

Strategic Intent
Defining a Sound Business Strategy and Business Model

It would seem obvious that every organization would have a strategic plan. However, many businesses do not have one. Hope is NOT a business plan but some businesses operate under this premise. Many organizations think their budget is their business plan. A budget is an operating plan; it's far from a business plan. Companies that actually do have a strategic plan don't always hit their targets. Why? I believe it is primarily because companies have been led to believe that a business plan can be created with a quick, two-day, offsite, strategic planning session. But, from my experience, that's simply impossible. Strategic planning is far too complex and elaborate to be done in a weekend retreat.

Organizations without a strategic plan will not only have trouble hitting their growth targets, they will likely have trouble developing a strong leadership program. Without a strong strategic plan in place, it is impossible to link leadership development with an organization's strategic intent. Without a sound business strategy that identifies a company's strategic intent, the leaders can become confused about what is important. If the vision, mission, and direction of the company are unclear or are in a constant state of flux, leaders are left trying to hit a moving target or guess at what to focus on. Probably the number one cause of business failure is poor decisions, and you can trace that back to my case studies of fallen leaders: they simply made poor decisions.

In my years of observing companies, people, performance, and results I have come to believe the following: Unless there is a common cause for people to rally around, most people will just wander around. When it comes to developing your strategic intent, knowing where you are going and how you are going to get there is crucial. There is an old adage, "You can't be all things to all people." In his book *Good to Great*, Jim Collins talks about the Hedgehog Theory: all too often companies fail to focus on what makes them money. What is the Hedgehog Concept? It's a similar axiom to the One Thing. Based on the famous essay by Isaiah Berlin, "The Hedgehog and the Fox," it describes how the world is divided into two types of people. The fox knows many things. The fox is a very cunning creature, able to devise a myriad of complex strategies to sneak attacks upon the hedgehog. The hedgehog knows one big thing, rolling up into a perfect little ball, thus becoming a sphere of sharp spikes, pointing outward in all directions. The hedgehog always wins despite the different tactics the fox uses.

If we look at this concept of strategic intent further, there are three distinct business models. The three distinct business models are identified in Porter's model of competitive differentiation. Michael Porter is the Bishop Williams Lawrence University Professor at Harvard Business School and is the director of the school's Institute for Strategy and Competitiveness. Even though we are talking about developing a leadership development program, his concept is worthy of discussion as we explore how strategic intent and leadership are related.

- Product Innovation (Apple)

- Customer Service and Customer Loyalty (Nordstrom)

- Operational Effectiveness and Cost Efficiency (Walmart)

For the leaders who work at these three vastly different organizations, their mission and vision are clearly defined because the strategic intent of the business is clearly defined. When running a business, you might be able to operate under two of the three business strategies listed here but it's harder to pull off all three. In the example of Apple, everyone knows that innovation is key and exploring technology is paramount. In Nordstrom's case, its differentiator is customer service and the leaders of Nordstrom's understand the vision and mission, so in turn their leadership competencies are developed in accordance with the company's strategic initiative. In the last example, it's no secret that Walmart has positioned itself as the low-cost provider, and so efficiency is how leaders must drive their leadership initiatives. You will be the most successful sticking to one model is Porter's premise.

Having developed a strong business model and identifying your strategic intent is still not enough. There also has to be a strong corporate culture that demands leaders develop into world class leaders. This creates the mind-set and motivation to develop the leadership qualities and skills necessary for successful leadership. It is important to understand how leaders shape and reinforce the corporate culture and the reciprocal influence of culture on leadership effectiveness and business results. For leaders who have greater clarity on the strategic intent and direction of the company, the choices they make will have greater impact on the bottom line.

■ Defining Corporate Culture—Why Is It Critical?

You can't just take it for granted and assume that having a business plan in place is all it takes in order to develop your leadership program. You also can't take for granted that having a leadership development program in place will enhance the quality of the leaders within your organization. You must also have a corporate culture that emulates your business plan. The old cliché, "talk the talk and walk the walk," is exactly what this means. If your corporate culture does not emphasize how you go about executing your business plan, you're likely to have trouble achieving success. To begin with, it starts at the top, and the CEO must embrace a corporate culture that embraces the philosophy of building a learning organization. That is only the start of building your corporate culture, but it is an essential one. Without that piece, people won't be held accountable for the learning and developing that they should be doing. On the other hand, when the expectation for continuous learning becomes part of your corporate culture, learning is more likely to take place at the level you need it to.

Do you know if your strategic intent and your corporate culture are in sync? If you are unsure of what your culture looks like and how to evaluate your corporate culture, here are some questions to help you frame your thinking.

- Do we have a corporate culture that supports people?

- Do we allow people to fail?

- Do we encourage people to take chances?

- Do we give them the tools to learn?

- Do we hold them accountable for their development?

- Do we involve them in the process?

- Do we teach managers how to coach?

- Do we have a culture of discipline and execution or an Idea of the Month?

- Do we operate from fear or fun?

If you are a global company, the questions must run deeper:

- Do we have national and international boundaries?

- Are we a global company or do we operate independently in global markets?

- What should a global company look like?

- What should our customers expect from a global company?

- Do we have enough cultural experience and knowledge to do business in each part of the world?

- How much do we know about each country's culture and values?

- What is our strategy for building long-lasting relationships in each global market?

- How will we deal with the differences and potential conflicts that could exist?

Corporate culture is a hard thing to measure and is subjective in nature as everyone's definition of culture varies. Your perception of your corporate culture is seen through your paradigm, and that may not be reality. Don't be blinded by your own paradigm.

Surveys can be an impactful way of taking the pulse of an organization and allowing you to find out what is happening across the broad spectrum of the company. An effective survey will help you get the lay of the land before you embark down the wrong path. Usually, your survey will be more accurate if you use a third-party vendor rather than conducting it yourself internally. To have the meaningful impact you seek, you should do the following when planning your survey:

- Set the stage to help people understand why you are doing the survey and what you hope to accomplish.

- Help your staff feel comfortable so they will be candid and not fear retribution for saying something that might be offensive.

- Share the results with the respondents. If you don't, they will not believe it's worth spending the time to take the survey and may not speak up in the future.

- Address and, at the very least, make the recommended changes that emerge from the information or explain why something cannot be done. You CANNOT ignore this. You must also let the entire organization see that you have listened *and* acted upon the results of the survey.

* Conduct the EXACT same survey in twelve to fourteen months to determine if the changes have taken hold and improvements were made. If you change the survey and do not ask the same questions in the same way, you cannot compare the results accurately and you will not be able to determine if your company has made improvements. It is imperative that you be willing to conduct the exact same survey a year after the first.

If you follow these principles, people will see you are fully committed to making improvements. Keep in mind the following powerful statement, "People support what they help create." Listening and engaging your people will pay dividends when you build an organization around employee engagement.

While following these principles is the right thing to do, it is important to understand that doing all these things does not guarantee you success. As an example, I was speaking to a president of a company about the employee feedback he tries to receive at the end of every month. All of the feedback he was getting was positive, yet there was a large increase in turnover from the previous year. To address the issue of staff departures, he brought in a third party to conduct employee interviews and found out that the reason people were leaving was because they were frustrated with several members of the senior leadership team. They told the president what he wanted to hear not what he *needed* to hear. This is not an uncommon situation, which is why surveys are more revealing when they are conducted by a third-party provider, especially if there are difficult leaders in place.

■ The Corporate Challenge—Are You Getting Results?

Leadership development must be part of the strategic initiative. Now that your corporate culture has been established and your strategic business plan is in place, you need to ask whether your leadership team is getting the results you want. If not, why not?

- Is it because your strategic business plan falls short?

- Is it because your corporate culture is not where it needs to be?

- Is it because you don't have a strong enough leadership development program to get there?

- Is it because you have the wrong leaders in place?

- Is it because you do not have the right people in the right positions?

- Is it because you have not established a set of leadership competencies?

- Is it all of the above?

- Is it something else? If so, then what is it?

As you begin to create your leadership development program, it is important to evaluate where you are today, where you have come from, and where you want to go. You may consider some type of survey or audit to help you get a baseline. If this is going to be a strategic corporate initiative, you need to audit what has worked and what hasn't worked in the past, as well as what you need to do going forward to help you avoid the same mistakes of the past.

Asking targeted questions can help you gain clarity on which direction to take. In every organization there are always projects that have been started but never completed or pursued. It is important NOT to succumb to the *Flavor of the Month* or the *Idea of the Month*. As you begin to lay the groundwork for creating your strategic leadership initiative, here are some questions to help you direct your thinking. Let's start by exploring the many corporate challenges you face with regard to growing your business:

- What business challenges do you face today?

- What will the dynamics be tomorrow? In five years?

- What is the depth of your bench strength?

- Are your managers able to address present and future challenges?

- What leadership competencies are required?

- What competencies need to be developed?

- Do your leaders have an effective development plan?

- Do you have an effective pipeline and succession plan?

The next set of questions that come into play raise questions about what objectives will be required to prepare your leaders for the future.

- What does strategic leadership preparation need to accomplish?

- What leadership skills are required for success?

- What does the profile of your successful leaders look like?

- What core values are required to achieve business results?

- How do you go about determining factors for evaluating up-and-coming talent?

- What leadership development strategies are lacking?

- What methods do you need to attract, develop, and retain top talent?

- What is the status of your leadership development program? Is it a world class program?

- What is the quality of your leaders, and what challenges do you face with them?

- Do you have the right leaders in place? If not, what is the plan?

- What does your pipeline look like?

- Do you have an effective succession plan?

In Closing

There are many questions you'll have to ask and answer. But armed with the answers, you will have the foundation necessary to create a world class leadership development program. Linking leadership with strategic intent is the basis for creating a successful, fully committed program. Without this critical link in place the rest of the components required to build a successful leadership development program will be difficult to achieve. The organization has to recognize and value leadership development as being worth the efforts, as well as prioritize it as a major objective.

4

Developing Leadership Competencies

Everyone knows that job descriptions define the expectations of a person within their particular position or role at an organization. The problem is that most job descriptions were written about the turn of the century and have been updated infrequently. I may be exaggerating a bit, but I suspect I'm not that far off. Furthermore, especially in today's 24/7 economy, as roles and responsibilities shift, job descriptions are constantly changing and evolving, making it harder to keep them up to date. At best this leaves most job descriptions wanting. There is an even bigger problem, though, because what is often missing from the job description is a list of defined job competencies.

Without defining a set of competencies, executives are left uncertain about what is important to pay attention to besides staying within a budget or hitting a profit target. Certainly a job description will help guide the executive's actions regarding what results are expected from him or her, but it's the competencies that help define how well the person structures his or her day-to-day decision making in terms of getting the job done. When someone first becomes a supervisor or manager, he or she needs to learn many competencies. One of the basic and essential skills is how to delegate work. While this may seem elementary, the truth is there are real challenges behind this seemingly simple competency. All the other competencies will also have their own set of challenges as well. To illustrate this, let's use delegating as an example. In a person's transition from managing himself to managing others, delegating becomes critical, but far too many managers have trouble doing this. Some people find it is easier and more comfortable to just do it themselves than to hand it off to someone else or teach someone else how to do it.

Most people do not realize this but it is often a behavioral problem that gets in the way of a competency. Behavior can be as much of the reason for poor delegating skills as much as it is a deficiency of the competency itself. Here is why. People who are perfectionists think it's easier to do a task themselves because no one will do it as thoroughly as they will, and this saves them time from having to do it over. Highly dominant people, who are typically as impatient as they are dominant, will just do it themselves because they can do it quicker with less hassle. In another example, building team unity is a competency that shy, introverted people will have a harder time with than outgoing, extroverted people. That is how mastering the skill itself as well as someone's behavior gets in the way. These two dynamics create a double-edged sword when it comes to mastering competencies. There are a significant number of competencies that our *Leadership Competency Inventory* can help you structure if you don't have something in place. Here are some of the major areas of competencies in our inventory. In each of these areas there are subcompetencies within each grouping, but this will give you an overview.

- Thinking Skills

- Interpersonal Skills

- Personal Skills

- Communication Skills

- Teamwork

- Leadership

As much as delegating can be impacted by behavior, it is also impacted by not mastering and understanding the competency itself. Consider this example. One of my clients promoted the quality control manager to the plant manager. As I was reviewing her assessment results with her, we discussed the fact that she was a very structured—not to mention a very controlling and self-reliant individual. She was used to doing everything herself, and in the new role she would really have to work on letting go of the day-to-day duties and focus on how to delegate effectively. After her first year in the role, we conducted a 360 review.

One of the areas in which she received poor marks was delegating. When we sat down to discuss her 360 results she said, "I don't understand why I got poor marks here. I remember you told me a year ago I needed to work on my delegating skills and I have worked very hard to make sure I delegate things to everyone." I asked her to tell me her approach and why she thought she was delegating things to others. Her reply was, "Every morning in our staff meeting I make sure everyone has their list of things that they have to get done."

There is a big difference between telling others what needs to get done and delegating work that others will complete. While this is a very simple example, it supports the premise that job competencies are a critical component in helping to define and shape the actions of anyone within their role. Competencies are not just for roles in management or leadership, either. Take the role of project manager. The role does not manage anyone but project management is just one of many competencies required to be successful in a variety of positions.

The list of competencies for any job is essential so that the individual can focus on the soft skills that will help them manage the role more effectively. More time will be devoted to a discussion on competencies and the aspect of soft skills and the role of leadership in chapter 7, "Three-Dimensional Leadership." Also, it's worth noting that not only is it important to develop a set of competencies, it is essential to create the training programs that help people develop them.

Linking Leadership Competencies with Strategic Intent

From a leadership perspective it is necessary to develop a set of leadership competencies that support the organization's strategic intent. What is often overlooked and misunderstood are two different areas in which competencies need to be addressed. The first is the most obvious: specific duties with a job description as I have just explained. The other is a list of competencies that define the corporate culture and the company's strategic intent. These are things every leader in the organization must follow. It is impossible to link your leadership initiatives with your strategic intent without a defined set of competencies at an organizational level. These leadership competencies define not only your strategic intent but your corporate culture.

The competencies for the various leadership roles for Apple are different than the competencies for the leadership roles in Walmart and are different from the leadership competencies for Nordstrom. That is because one company focuses on technology and innovation, one focuses on operational efficiencies, and the other focuses on fashion and customer service. There are significant differences in these three companies that warrant different leadership competencies. However, even though there are fundamental differences in these three companies, a common thread that could be a leadership competency in each of them would be championing diversity or forward planning. Giving the executives the parameters to which they are held accountable through a defined set of competencies helps them to understand the way they must lead. If an executive cannot understand and deliver to a defined set of competencies, then he or she is likely to have a hard time managing the day-to-day role to achieve a company's strategic intent. Here is an example of what a set of leadership competencies might look like. Refer to the graph in Figure 4.1 as well.

- Achieve Business Results

- Forward Planning

- Build Customer Loyalty

- Strengthen Internal and External Partnerships

- Champion Diversity

- Manage Change and Encourage Adaptability

- Lead and Coach Others

- Self-Management

It is a given that leaders need to understand the results they are asked to achieve. Not defining a set of leadership competencies leads to confusion about what is important for the leader. Rather than just making decisions that affect the bottom line only, or to meet an expected budget, they can make better decisions based on the leadership competencies that support the culture and the strategic intent of the business. By doing so the executives can measure themselves against the expectations of the organization, and the organization can measure the success of the executives because there is a defined set of criteria in which to evaluate the leaders' work.

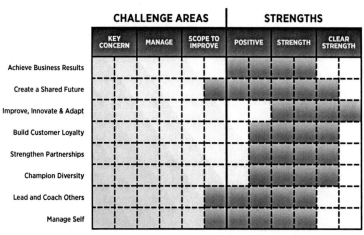

OVERALL DIAGNOSTIC PROFILE

Figure 4.1 Overall Diagnostic Profile–Identify
Areas for Improvement and Strengths

A compelling reason to define a set of leadership competencies is because people are creatures of habit and are most comfortable within their own areas of expertise. Furthermore, their actions are often driven by their behavior. When this happens, the leader can become unbalanced and stuck in his or her own paradigm. If one of the leadership competencies is forward planning and the leader is cautious, conservative risk-averse, and is better at the day-to-day aspects of managing the role, the forward planning and strategic planning will suffer. Then, decisions are often made based on a person's personality and lack of skills in this area. This will be addressed in more detail in chapter 11, "The Unknown Element - Human Behavior and Its Impact on Leadership."

Look at the progression of a bookkeeper who becomes an accountant, then becomes the accounting manager, then the controller, then the vice president of finance, then CFO, and then president. The organization may focus too much on the financial health of the organization and miss other opportunities. If you're an accountant, you may be saying, "So what's so wrong with that notion?" Exactly! Another example is the lathe operator who becomes the shift supervisor, then becomes the plant superintendent, then becomes plant manager, and then becomes vice president of operations and then becomes president. The higher you go in terms of responsibility, the more soft skills are needed and the less hard skills come into play. These competencies and soft skills are needed to lead effectively but, more importantly, the leader must be willing to dig deeply and honestly enough into his or her own skills to identify any gaps.

To give this example further relevance, imagine what the business looks like when the VP of operations becomes president, versus the CFO who becomes president, versus the VP of sales who becomes president versus the VP of engineering who becomes president. There are likely to be four very different organizations. That is because the business will be run based on the executive's paradigm, comfort level, and area of expertise. The odds will increase that the business will be unbalanced, meaning the state of the business may be too heavily weighted in the area of the leader's expertise and comfort zone. A set of corporate competencies are needed to help assure the decisions the leaders make on a day-to-day basis are in line with the strategic intent of the business overall. It's hard to tell, but similar dynamics were probably a contributing factor in the downfall of the executives at Coca-Cola, Mattel, and Enron.

As we move from managing ourselves as an individual contributor and move into a role of managing others, things change. Our next role becomes managing managers who manage managers, and so on. At each new level the role we take on has more responsibility along with a new set of competencies that require another degree of knowledge and expertise. Each phase represents a major change to the very core of who we are. Those changes include understanding the differences at each level in various areas. To succeed we must accept that more is required of us as we rise up the ranks and there are likely to be topics in which we need to expand, grow, and improve. These matters would include:

- New work values

- New time horizons

- New applications

- New skill requirements

- New thinking skills

- New competencies

These are not the same skills that got us our first promotion. These changes include learning a new set of competencies as well as a deeper grasp of the competencies we learned at every turn. It becomes necessary to develop a set of competencies, and those competencies need to align with an organization's strategic intent. This is the point at which the leaders of the organization align with the strategy of the organization and whether or not they are executing the mission and living up to the values of the organization. A successful leadership development program will link its leadership competencies with its corporate culture and its strategic intent.

These are the integrated knowledge, skills, judgment, and attributes that people need to perform a job effectively. Having a defined set of competencies for each role in your business will show employees the kind of behaviors the organization values, and which competencies are required to help achieve corporate objectives. Not only can your team members work more effectively and achieve their potential by understanding what competencies they need to master, there are many business benefits from linking personal performance with corporate goals and values. Competencies provide ways to measure an individual's ability and also offer ways to help the executive understand what he or she needs to learn. A set of competencies is in fact a management tool. The following statement speaks to the concept of measurements:

What doesn't get measured doesn't get managed and what doesn't get managed doesn't get measured.

It's that way with competencies. What are the competencies that differentiate a supervisor from a manager or a leader? How are they measured? How are they monitored? They will never be measured or monitored if they haven't been clearly defined. It is essential to find the right way to define the skills, behaviors, and attitudes that workers need to perform their roles effectively. How do you know they're qualified for the job? In other words, how do you know what to measure? I used delegating as an example earlier, but let's take a look at another competency called "business acumen."

As someone moves up through the levels of the organization, various levels of business acumen become essential. The first phase is often that of budgetary responsibility which develops into full profit and loss (P&L) responsibility. The business acumen for a bookkeeper is different than it is for a controller. There is also a difference between the business acumen required by a plant manager and a controller, and even a CFO or CEO. Business acumen as a competency then goes from the basics of budgetary responsibilities up to the skill set of conducting a turnaround, developing a strategic plan, overseeing mergers and acquisitions, and even expanding a company internationally. You could enlarge these competencies more to include taking a private company public or a public company private. All of these competencies are related to business acumen and they go from the most basic to the most sophisticated. To have them identified within the corporate culture that in turn defines the strategic intent of the business cannot be overlooked and is essential to developing your leadership competencies. In turn, these competencies are an integral part of a successful world class leadership development program.

The Competency Framework

Creating a competency model is an essential way to create a methodology to evaluate, monitor, and measure the skills, abilities, attributes, and knowledge of people in your organization. The framework allows you to measure current competency levels to make certain your staff has the expertise needed to add value to the business.

It also helps managers make informed decisions about talent recruitment, retention, and succession strategies. By identifying the behaviors and skills needed for each role, you're able to budget and plan for the training and development your company really needs. The process of creating a competency framework is long and complex. To ensure a successful outcome, you should involve employees in different roles to evaluate jobs and explain actual workplace situations. The increased level of understanding and the linkage between individual roles and organizational performance makes the effort well worth it.

Defining which competencies are necessary for success in your organization can help you do the following:

- Ensure that your people demonstrate sufficient expertise.

- Recruit and select new staff more effectively.

- Evaluate performance more effectively.

- Identify skill and competency gaps more efficiently.

- Provide more customized training and professional development, and

- Plan sufficiently for succession.

Here are some tips for implementing the framework:

- **Link to business objectives.** Make connections between individual competencies and organizational goals and values as much as possible.

- **Reward the competencies.** Check that your policies and practices support and reward the competencies identified.

- **Provide coaching and training.** Make sure there is adequate coaching and training available. People need to know that their efforts to grow and develop will be supported.

- **Keep it simple.** Design the framework to be as simple as possible. You want the document to be used, not filed away and forgotten.

- **Communicate.** Most importantly, treat the implementation as you would any other change initiative. The more open and honest you are throughout the process, the better the end result and the better the chances of the project achieving your objectives.

In Closing

Very early in my career when I received my first branch/sales management role I was responsible for ordering the inventory, getting the building permits, dealing with the floor plan at the bank, handling the marketing for the branch, and hiring the staff—not to mention my main focus, driving sales results. In fact I hired my first two salespeople, both of whom I terminated in the first year. I was about as prepared for that new role as a new pitcher in the majors. The competencies that I lacked could fill the Library of Congress. And while I make light of this, its truism takes on relevance in every person who takes the next step in their career and their next assignment. As evidence of this truism, and at yet another turn in my career I became president of a $75 million company. Even though I had been part of merger and acquisition (M&A) teams in other companies, I soon realized I did not possess the depth of M&A experience necessary to effectively lead M&A activity in my new position. I guess that's why they call it *experience* and it comes from the school of hard knocks. So it goes for every newly promoted individual; often, it is trial by fire and we wind up managing from a disadvantage instead of an advantage. We are then predisposed and guilty of the management premise, Ready-Fire-Aim. The higher we climb the less prepared we often are and the more we will realize our own ignorance.

It doesn't have to be that way! By understanding the competencies necessary for success at every level and then mastering them, leaders can help define their own success. Without a defined set of leadership competencies, leadership can be like "fishing in the dark." The organization has to define these leadership competencies, create the training and developmental components necessary, and then prepare the leader for leadership development. Leadership competencies must be an integral part of every successful leadership development program.

5

Creating an Internal Feedback Loop

Setting the stage for executive development requires that the executive receives honest and direct feedback. To be truly effective it is essential the feedback comes from multiple perspectives. In addition, if the feedback will have any significance, it must be acted on. Unfortunately, it is not unusual for someone to receive feedback and revert back to his or her previous behavior and actions. It happens all the time. It's like someone who goes on a diet. Diets never work long-term, but changing your lifestyle and eating habits does. The same can be said for executive development. To accomplish a successful outcome in executive development requires an internal feedback process that provides insight for the executive from multiple perspectives, not just the person's immediate manager.

To understand how to create a successful outcome as a result of that feedback, there are some fundamental guidelines that will help ensure the feedback is relevant and impactful:

- Feedback must be sponsored and driven from the top down.

- It cannot be solely driven by HR.

- Feedback must have the executive's best interests in mind.

- Conditions that encourage and support people will only work with those who want to improve.

- Learning does not occur unless it is sparked by a person's own interest and curiosity.

- Learning will thrive if it is tied into someone's own vision, desires, and objectives.

If you expect your leaders to grow and emerge into successful leaders, you must have an internal feedback loop in place. The reasons are too significant to ignore, which makes the case for having a world class leadership development program in place not only important but essential so nothing that would shortchange the program is omitted. The main reason is simple: people *need* feedback. The good news is, most want it and some even crave feedback. There are a select few who don't care to hear it. They need others to help them see what they can't see in themselves or for themselves. The real goal of an internal feedback loop is to help give the executive the needed perspective from others. If he cannot see it for himself, nothing is going to change.

The higher an individual rises in an organization the less feedback he receives. People become shielded from the real feedback they need. The possibility also exists that the higher they go within the organization, the less likely they want to receive feedback. The most common reason is they feel they don't need feedback. Recall the case studies from the chapter on our executives from Coca-Cola, Mattel, and Enron. What if those executives had received feedback on their performances sooner?

As executives climb the corporate ladder, there are many new skills, competencies, and behaviors they need to learn along the way, but often they never acquire these new capabilities. Furthermore, as executives move higher in the organization, they become less and less exposed to honest feedback from their direct reports and colleagues. Their title and position isolates them and makes them unreachable and even untouchable. In fact, it is the title and position that can boost executives' ego so much that they lose sight of their own work and perspective. It's not only their title that can get in their way, their ego can and, more often than not, does. When ego and titles collide the outcome is compounded. Those in the top spots are the least likely to receive feedback simply because of the position they hold. In fact, they are often the ones who need it the most but rarely seek it and, to make matters worse, may believe they don't need it. Likewise, they are the ones who could benefit the most and, in the process, set a good example for leadership development throughout the organization.

When the executive is the owner/president of the company, or if the president is a family member of a family-owned company, you have an even more challenging situation. People simply will not cross the line when asked to provide honest feedback when there are challenges at the top. How many executives really challenge the president of the company? That's why having the president fully on board and personally engaged with the leadership development process is essential. The president must be willing to go through the same process the leadership team will go through. This is also where a third-party advisor and executive coach can have a huge impact.

There are those executives who just don't see that they need to change. Then there are those that may not need to change dramatically but instead would benefit from developing new skills, new competencies, and new behaviors. At every new stage in the progression of an executive's roles, there are new skills, values, and processes necessary to fully master the new position. However, when an executive ABSOLUTELY believes that he or she doesn't need or have to change, then any attempt to get the person to change is unlikely to bear fruit. Unfortunately, and all too often, the person believes that the traits she possesses are what made her successful and are responsible for her promotion. Now that she's in a senior role, she may believe she is in that role because of what she has done and how she has acted in the past. She may say, "Why would I possibly need to change? Who I am is what got me where I am." The bottom line is the person doesn't see any need to change and then rest assured they won't.

People in any position are prone to have blind spots. This becomes more and more problematic when someone assumes greater responsibilities. The person simply doesn't see any shortcoming or even worse, believes he or she doesn't have any faults. Think about this statement: *A man won over against his will is of the same opinion still.*

What this statement means is no matter how much you try to twist someone's arm, and no matter how much pressure you put on someone to help him see his blind spots and what he needs to change, a shift is only going to happen when he sees it for himself, accepts them, and commits to work on making changes. We call this moving from self-insight to self-management, and it's a significant shift that is integral to the development process.

Once people are willing to focus on self-management and hold themselves accountable for their own actions and their own development, only then will personal growth and change begin to take place. You cannot just will it upon them. If they don't see a need to change, they aren't going to change. This is why it is imperative to develop a strong internal feedback loop that allows employees to receive honest feedback from multiple outlets and multiple perspectives. The problem is that usually people don't provide the most honest feedback. People are fearful of saying what may need to be said; they're worried about losing their job or alienating themselves from colleagues for voicing criticism or a negative comment. This is especially true when the person needing the feedback is the president, a family member, or someone who has close ties to the chief executive.

Here are several strategies and related tactics to generate valid and useful feedback regarding the performance and effectiveness of your leaders. It will be difficult to achieve any level of significant success if any of these components are left out. In other words, if you shortchange the process you short change the initiative and your results will be less than the desired outcome.

■ Performance Reviews

The most common and the most obvious internal feedback loop is the annual performance review. These often fall short of delivering optimal results because they are one-on-one conversations with the direct manager. If the individual does not respect his manager or disagrees with his evaluation, the feedback is unlikely to have an impact on leadership development. Another possibility is that the manager isn't an effective manager, and never confronts a problem situation, so the employee never receives any useful feedback. Without feedback or guidance, the employee won't develop new skills or behaviors.

Unfortunately, most managers are not skilled enough themselves to aid in an executive's development to any significant extent. Even if managers have taken part in a coaching program does not mean they are equipped to handle everything involved in coaching someone else. This is why performance reviews will not likely yield true leadership development and why additional feedback from multiple perspectives is needed. The feedback from the performance review does have relevance in the overall leadership development process, but it just may not carry enough weight based on the traditional performance appraisal model that happens once a year. This is one of the main reasons why there is a shift in the performance management system in many companies, as the feedback is ongoing and is without a rating system in some cases.

■ Assessment Reviews

Another way to provide feedback is by using some type of an assessment process. Feedback you get from doing an assessment can help you begin to think about self-development. There are a number of assessment programs available but, ideally, you want to use one that can serve multiple purposes. You want a system that will help with executive development across organizational lines. It isn't practical to have different assessment programs in use at various levels of your organization. It is preferable to use one assessment that can serve selection, coaching, and leadership to create a common language throughout your organization. Only the more sophisticated assessments can accomplish this.

There is such a wide array of assessments to choose from that, unless you are extremely well-versed in this field, it can become very confusing. Because of their complexity, I have devoted chapter 6, "Exploring the World of Assessments," to this subject. I will explain how you can distinguish between a simple assessment and a sophisticated assessment and why it's important to understand what differentiates them. In addition, providing feedback to an executive about his results needs to come from someone who understands the assessments and how to use them in the feedback and coaching process. This is far too critical a skill to be handled by an inexperienced employee.

■ Peer Interviews

There is value in using peer interviews, and I highly recommend them. Peer interviews often reveal more than a 360 can reveal. When used alongside the 360 they are very powerful. However, when done by internal resources, they are not always effective. People are sometimes unwilling to trust an internal process because they fear their comments may hurt them in the future. Conducting a peer interview is far more effective when using a third-party provider who is interviewing an employee than having an employee provide his or her own written comments.

In most 360 assessments there is usually a section where the individual completing the review can write comments. This rarely happens because of the reluctance of people to say things for fear of retribution, let alone providing written comments that could be redirected back to them. I myself have witnessed far more revealing results from peer interviews than the actual 360 themselves.

■ 360-Degree Assessments

By definition, a 360-degree assessment is when an individual answers a series of questions about how the person rates their own performance in their particular position. In addition, the employee's manager, peers, and subordinates also answer the same questions about how they see the executive's performance. The objective is to compare the self-perception of the executive with those who work with and around the executive.

I am a huge proponent of the 360 process. Unfortunately, the vast majority of the 360-degree assessments that are conducted fail to produce the desired results. There are a few reasons why the traditional 360 process has its flaws. The objective of the process is to use the 360 assessment to create a powerful coaching outcome with the executive that prioritizes the true learning experiences to deliver successful outcomes. Before I discuss the process and how to achieve a successful outcome, I want you to read the "Top 10 Reasons for Rejecting Your 360." I don't know its origin, and I don't know if David Letterman had a hand in developing this list, but these comical statements are actually rather accurate.

Top 10 Reasons for Rejecting Your 360

 # 10 My job makes me act that way; I'm REALLY not like that.

 # 9 This was just a bad time to ask for feedback.

 # 8 All my strengths are correct, but my weaknesses are not.

 # 7 Everyone has it in for me.

 # 6 I used to be that way, but I've changed recently.

 # 5 Nobody understands what I'm going through.

 # 4 This must be someone else's report.

 # 3 My raters did not understand the questions.

 # 2 They're all jealous of my success.

 # 1 Oh, I agree, it's all accurate, but I JUST DON'T CARE!

While there is comic relief in the Top 10 model, there is relevance to each and every statement. A well-designed 360-degree evaluation is used as a feedback tool and therefore should include relevant topics so the executive can begin to identify where their gaps are as they relate to the competencies they need to develop for their particular role. While I am a huge proponent of the 360 process, my experience has proven that, more often than not, this process doesn't typically fulfill its intended objectives. The following are organizational factors that severely limit the validity and effectiveness of traditional 360 assessments.

The Down Side—Why 360s Don't Work

- The 360-degree assessments are treated as an event rather than part of an ongoing corporate process that is deemed important.

- The executive is being singled out and identified as a problem employee.

- All the executives are going through the process because there is one particular executive who is problematic, and the organization does not want to call attention to that individual, so everyone goes through the process, which dilutes the purpose.

- The 360 is used as an executive leadership development component. Once completed, the executive checks it off his list saying, "Yes, I did that!" and moves on to the next objective, doing nothing more with the information.

- While reading through a 360 report, the executive focuses on trying to determine who made the comments, instead of the value and content of the comments themselves, thereby missing the intended purpose of the process altogether and essentially shooting the messenger.

- True and honest feedback is not given due to fear of retribution (especially true for aggressive executives, owners, CEOs, presidents, senior-level executives, and family members) and nothing gets brought to the surface. Again, this is defeating the whole purpose of the 360 process.

* The employee is not given any advance explanation on how to decipher the results.

* No follow-up is provided to hold individuals accountable for self-development.

* There is no motivation to change and no consequences if change does not take place in the future.

* No clear direction or plan is set in place on how to get started and utilize the information.

* No mentor or coach to support the executive is provided to help the executive make sense of the results, let alone move that information into action plans.

There are ways, however, to make a 360 work. By paying attention to the dos and don'ts, you can create a 360 process that will provide a return on the time and money invested to assure a successful outcome. Here are some specifics that should help you have more effective 360 processes.

The Upside–How to Make 360s Work

* Create an open culture of trust so people believe the results will be used in a professional manner.

- Support and reinforce the process from the top down.

- Emphasize and ensure the confidentiality of responses and results by using a third-party administrator to conduct the 360 rather than using internal processes.

- Encourage open, honest, and thorough responses.

- Set deadlines for respondents as well as for the person being assessed.

- Follow through by creating a written clear and concise development plan.

- Set a timeline for assessing progress moving forward.

- Conduct a second 360 in eight to ten months to evaluate progress.

- Hold people accountable for making changes and improvements.

In order for a 360-degree assessment to have the greatest impact, it is imperative for the individual going through the 360 process to be highly active in the process. There is a need for the executive's commitment and buy-in. The executive must be fully engaged and committed at an emotional level for self-improvement. The individual has a stake in the process and will be rewarded if he uses the information in the way in which it is intended. The following tips will help frame the individual's role in the 360 process and hopefully instill self-directed learning.

The Individual's Role in the 360 Process

- Be open to the process and the results.

- Be an active participant.

- Be honest with yourself.

- Don't just ask your friends to give feedback; make sure you include people who will tell you what you need to hear, not only what you want to hear.

- Include those participants with whom you work with on a regular basis who can objectively evaluate your performance.

- Invite people to provide candid and honest feedback.

- Be a driving force in your development plan.

- Commit to a willingness to learn and grow.

- Meet deadlines set forth in your development plan.

- Find an executive coach who can help you develop new skill sets.

- Meet with your manager and/or coach regularly to discuss your progress.

- Don't try and figure out who said what and don't judge the information. Instead, listen to what it reveals about you and take it to heart.

- Thank those you asked to participate for their feedback.

- **Above all: don't shoot the messenger.**

■ Executive Coaching

Another way to provide a feedback loop incorporates the use of an executive coach. This option is often the best alternative because there are advantages to using an external coach. For a detailed discussion of coaches and the coaching process, read chapter 9.

In Closing

Honest and direct feedback sets the stage for executive development, and it is essential that it comes from multiple perspectives to be the most effective. Performance reviews, assessment reviews, and peer reviews, along with integrating a robust 360-degree assessment, are among the many ways you can create a robust internal feedback process. Incorporating all of them will go a long way toward building a world class leadership development program. More importantly, it will help you develop world class leaders and create a consistent approach to leadership development.

CHAPTER

6

Exploring the World of Assessments
Differentiating the Simple from the Sophisticated

Guess or Assess! Assessments are a KEY component in evaluating and understanding people's behavior and play an integral part in assessing and developing leaders. The right assessments can reveal how people cope when faced with challenges, demonstrate their level of emotional resolve, self-awareness, and level of emotional intelligence. Assessments can also be used to show the depth of a person's critical thinking skills and problem-solving ability. This insight about an individual's personality, behavior, emotional intelligence, and critical thinking skills is essential not only to support the leadership development and succession planning process, but also to serve as an integral part of the selection process. You can't afford to make a bad hire and you cannot pick out problematic behaviors from an interview. In the selection process an external candidate is relatively unknown because there is no baseline like you would have from an employee within your organization. Understanding and using the right assessment tool can give you more insight into key behaviors as well as those problematic behaviors you are unable to uncover in other ways. Likewise, understanding and using the right assessment tool is an important aspect of a highly successful leadership development program as well as a world class selection program.

Let me emphasize that this chapter is more technical than others in the book. This is necessary because of the complexity of this subject. The material here will help you understand the differences and nuances among the majority of assessments available on the market. You will realize that the vast majority of assessments cannot delve deeply enough into personality and behavior to provide the depth of information necessary to support the talent management process and the organization's leadership development initiatives. In chapter 5, I discussed the value of using assessments as part of the feedback process for executive development. The information here will help provide more insight into that process and show you how to distinguish the differences between the simple and the sophisticated assessments.

It is unfortunate, but there is no rating service for assessments. The auto industry has its J. D. Power and Associates, but there is no such resource that compares and contrasts assessments. The main body of knowledge rests with the Buros Institute's *Mental Measurements Yearbook*, the independent review source for finding any information about a particular assessment. Any independent review of various assessments is valuable only to the degree to which the test publisher is willing to provide its validation and reliability studies. As you will learn, some test organizations aren't willing to release this data. While there are resources that critique various assessments, there is no resource that compares one assessment to another. My goal here is to review the key components of assessments so that you understand which one is best for your purposes.

Many people are unaware that the vast majority of assessments cannot fully assess a person's personality to really be effective in supporting the talent management and leadership development initiatives, let alone use them as an element of a dynamic selection model. Most people are predisposed to continue using a tool with which they're already familiar. Chances are they're using an assessment that isn't measuring what they need it to do and they're not even aware of this shortcoming. Any assessment, and I mean any, will hit the mark and be spot on in what it will reveal about yourself and anyone else. When people read their assessment results from the Myers-Briggs/MBTI or any other, nine out of ten people agree that it is reflective of who they are. The DiSC, Birkman, Predictive Index/PI, Profiles XT, Caliper, MBTI, and all the others will all be spot on with the data. Why? These tests measure what they say they will measure and, because they are all validated, meaning they will measure the traits they claim to measure, there is more than a 90 percent possibility that you will identify with the report you read.

This is a really important point to understand about assessments. It is not what an assessment tells you; it is what it *doesn't* tell you. What I mean by this is that almost every assessment report on the market produces what I call "soft language." This means that it mainly presents all the pertinent behavioral data in a positive light and is expressed in such a way that it is difficult to tell if there is any problematic behavior present.

The next thing to understand even beyond that point is what an assessment *can't* tell you. What this means is that some assessments do not measure certain traits that others do. Therefore, you will discover why I say it is what an assessment *can't* tell you that is an important distinction. This will become more understandable as I explain this in more detail later on. This information is critical because of its significant impact on using assessments for leadership development.

One of the interesting things I have observed is that some organizations are so entrenched with the assessments they use currently that even when they find out their current tool isn't sufficient they don't want the hassle and inconvenience of introducing a new assessment or changing midstream. I've seen this reaction several times. If you are going to use an assessment for leadership development or even selection, you must recognize how you're using it and its strengths and limitations. If it's not providing the information you need, you must change to another system. If assessments can provide additional feedback to an executive for development and can help an organization gain an understanding of an executive's capabilities and potential, then using them should be a logical thing to do. That means that the assessments and the process you use should be highly capable of predicting an individual's behavior, and their critical thinking skills as well. The problem is very few people understand the difference between a simple versus a sophisticated instrument and what the differences are between them as to what is measured. That is why you must differentiate between the various assessments that are available. Doing so requires someone who knows what questions to ask about a particular assessment test.

I have studied and researched assessments for nearly thirty years. I have been using them in my practice since 1991, and I have conducted nearly 13,000 assessments in my career. Over the years, in my work helping organizations build a selection and leadership development model, I have realized that using assessments is one of the most misinformed, misunderstood, and underutilized areas in the talent management and organizational development process. I also have evidence they are just as misunderstood in the selection process, probably even more so. It is this firsthand experience that has led me to know how to differentiate and understand the differences between assessments. That is what I hope to teach you so you know which assessments you should be using and why. I will also help you see their connection to leadership development, talent management, and selection. I use the example of and the term "assessments" because using just one, more often than not, is not enough to evaluate and assess the talents and abilities of an individual.

A properly used assessment process can open up a dialogue with an individual about his behavior and tendencies which may be negatively impacting his work performance. This information would not be evident in a conversation because people with extreme egos, and especially those with narcissistic tendencies, do not like to talk about their weaknesses. Some people don't think they have any weaknesses while others aren't willing to admit to having them. Then there are those individuals who are just simply in denial. Therefore, using assessments in the process of leadership development and especially executive coaching is essential.

Understanding Critical Thinking Skills

Beyond measuring behavior and emotional intelligence, it is also necessary to evaluate and measure the depth of a person's critical thinking skills and problem-solving ability. While this chapter is about utilizing assessments to evaluate personality, behavior, and emotional intelligence, it is important to discuss the use of assessments to measure critical thinking skills. As an individual advances in an organization, the more essential critical thinking skills, problem solving, and intelligence become. Often, the lack of effective problem-solving skills is a derailing factor for an executive and a contributing factor to the Peter Principle. We can use our leadership examples from Coca-Cola, Mattel, and Enron as classic examples of the Peter Principle.

To help you get a baseline to measure critical thinking skills, there are a number of different assessments that measure various types of intelligence. Just like personality assessments, not all problem-solving assessments measure the same things. Perceptual reasoning is one form of intelligence that can be measured but is rarely done. Perceptual reasoning is an individual's natural ability and it is often referred to as IQ or intelligence quotient. The reason is it rarely done is because to accurately measure this you must proctor this particular assessment because there are four timed tests as part of the test itself. Today people want an online process that is quick and efficient and this one is time-consuming and cannot be done online. The mean score for IQ is 100 for the general population. A person's perceptual reasoning is independent of education, gender, or ethnic background. In one of our leadership studies with eighty high potential managers, the mean score for the group for IQ was 110. This means that the average high potential manager was 10 points above the mean.

There are only a handful of behavior and personality assessments on the market that include some sort of critical thinking or problem-solving skills component within their assessment. There is one test that has an IQ component that measures perceptual reasoning and that is the Culture Fair. A true IQ test is a separate test in and of itself and uses spatial recognition, not words or numerical reasoning. Neither the MBTI, DiSC, nor Predictive Index/PI, to name a few types of assessments, has any problem-solving component embedded within them, let alone a perceptual reasoning or IQ component. Later in this chapter I will discuss the 16PF® Questionnaire, one of the more sophisticated assessments on the market. It is the primary instrument of choice in our assessment model. It has a problem-solving component within the assessment, which is as reliable as the behavioral portion. It is not a perceptual reasoning/IQ test; it is a verbal and numerical reasoning test. When we administer our executive battery we include a complete perceptual reasoning test. While it is valid and reliable in predicting a person's problem-solving ability it does have its limitations. It measures a person's ability to solve math problems and analogies where all the needed information is included and it does provide some insight into the person's problem-solving ability. However, the 16PF Questionnaire does not measure other kinds of problem solving that other cognitive assessments do. That is why we use several different cognitive assessments.

When we evaluate more senior-level hires or conduct internal evaluations, where critical thinking is an essential part of the role, we use three additional assessments that measure different forms of intelligence and problem solving as part of our managerial and executive assessment batteries. These added tests are always used in our leadership development and selection model for higher-level positions for selection, development, coaching, or promotion. These three additional tests include one that measures IQ (perceptual reasoning), another measures inductive and deductive reasoning (indicates how well they apply logic to solving problems), and the other measures rate of speed of processing and learning agility. These three additional assessments help us gain a full awareness of an executive's critical thinking skills, problem-solving ability, perceptual reasoning, and intelligence, regardless of the position.

The Significance of Behavior and Performance

Behavior is the single biggest predictor of performance more than job skills, experience, education, and even critical thinking skills. While the other factors are relevant and have a bearing on job success—especially in higher-level roles, where critical thinking skills and intelligence come into play—behavior weighs in the most. Recall the failed executives mentioned in chapter 1 and you can see that some underlying behaviors had as much to do with their downfall as their lack of competencies and judgment. In addition to behavior, people's emotional intelligence is a critical factor. It is important to understand how they manage their emotions, cope with stressful situations, interact with people, and how much self-insight they have about their behavior, both good and bad. There are only a handful of assessments that can measure and uncover these traits in depth.

Assessments and Leadership Development

Assessments can add value and have an impact in opening up a dialogue with individuals about their strengths, weaknesses, and personality traits. Often, when people see the results from their own assessment, they are more open to conversation about themselves, especially if the results are favorable. It's when they aren't so favorable that it becomes interesting to observe them. Still, many people will remain guarded. This is one of the reasons why feedback from multiple perspectives is critical. Often the issues that surface from performance reviews and 360-degree assessment reviews will correlate to a person's assessment results. A word of caution is in order: providing feedback to someone from their assessment results can have a negative impact. The dynamics of the results and feedback should come from someone who has the qualifications and experience to explain the content and answer questions in an appropriate professional manner.

Insight–What Can Be Revealed?

Here is an example of how an assessment can provide further insight about someone. In a conversation with an HR manager, we were discussing an individual's need for some executive coaching. The discussion revolved around the person being full of himself and also becoming stressed and emotional. If this is the case it would not be a surprise to find that a 360 assessment and peer interviews would produce the same information. If the person's assessment results reveal that he needs to be the center of attention, is overly dominant, and has a low tolerance for stress, you can begin to create the feedback loop to help him see what he can't see for himself and may need to work on. The proper assessment and, more importantly, a battery of quality assessments can help assess the difference between someone who is full of himself because he is smarter than other people and needs to see how innocent celebrations might make others see him as egotistical, versus someone who is truly egotistical and needs to be reminded of his imperfections. There are only a handful of assessments that can make the distinction between the two. The more sophisticated assessments can provide this kind of valuable information and measure any extreme behaviors that may be problematic and potentially derail an executive. In chapter 12, "Case Studies," I provide examples that show how you can combine various assessments to gain this powerful information. The case studies will reveal how utilizing a battery of assessments (several assessments that complement one another) can point to areas of concern that otherwise might go undetected.

Another advantage to using a more sophisticated assessment is that you have the added value of predicting future job success that will support the succession planning process. This is not something that can be achieved using any of the four-dimensional assessments that will be discussed later in this chapter. In one of the case studies I detail in chapter 12, we cautioned a client about promoting an individual. The assessments showed that while this employee was gifted, her talents would likely be overshadowed by some very difficult challenges present within her behavior. The client did, in fact, promote this individual only to terminate her within six months. In the detailed case study, you will see how our evaluation was able to predict the outcome by utilizing the results of the assessment.

Assessments can also be used to identify high-potential individuals as you build your leadership pipeline and determine succession plans. To get at the heart of professional development, using a battery of assessments can help executives target their own personal gaps to aid in their professional development. In order to do this effectively, it is important to understand why using a battery of assessments is highly essential and extremely beneficial to assess an individual's true talent. Using a highly validated and reliable instrument is essential but, more importantly, utilizing one that truly measures the depth of a person's personality is just as critical. As I have already mentioned, the challenge is that not very many assessments have the ability to reach deeply into relevant aspects of behavior that can derail a person's career and also carry a high degree of validity and reliability.

■ Understanding Validity and Reliability

It is essential to understand the significance between validity and reliability and why they are both important to understand when determining whether you are using a simple assessment or a sophisticated assessment. What is interesting to note is the only question people ask about is validity. It is the most common question that surfaces when the subject of assessments comes up. This is because most people don't understand enough about assessments to ask meaningful questions. All assessments really are validated. I have not found one yet that wasn't. So the response to the question is yes. But the more important query is, "to what degree and by whom?" While I'm going to address the aspect of validity, it is just as important to address reliability to help you understand why this is as critical to understand as validity. While validity and reliability are both important there are many more aspects of a quality assessment that you will come to learn that go beyond these two terms. The two go hand in hand, but they are not one in the same when it comes to differentiating the simple from the more sophisticated assessments.

Technically speaking, it is rare that an assessment on the market has not been validated. In other words, does it measure what it says it measures? There are different degrees of validity that you will come to learn as well. The bigger question is: "To what degree have they been validated and how deeply have they been tested?" There are some assessments that I call "homegrown," meaning they were developed in-house by a company for its own use. There are also some that were developed by someone, usually a psychologist, who wanted to develop his or her own brand. Here is where you really need to be careful because the odds are the psychologist does not have a team of experts to support and maintain the ongoing studies necessary to keep it current. If you are using a particular assessment and Buros Institute's *Mental Measurements Yearbook* has not critiqued it, you need to be very vigilant in regards to its validity and reliability. If you ask your assessment provider if its instrument is validated, the odds are high you will get a yes. If you ask if it's reliable and they say yes, they should be able to tell you the test-to-retest coefficient. If they don't know what this means and don't know what it is, the response should tell you the provider doesn't understand the difference. These terms are not one and the same, and it is important to understand the distinction when it comes to selecting not only an assessment but a vendor.

What most people do not realize is that many, if not all, assessment instruments are validated. The problem arises when assessments are validated only by the people who own and developed them and not by an independent review board. For an assessment to be validated, the review really needs to come from an outside third party, not from the company which produced the assessment. Imagine if a car manufacturer conducted its own crash tests and published its results instead of the Insurance Institute for Highway Safety, or letting BP determine if its drilling operations are safe. Think of it as a company that audits its own financials rather than using an outside, independent accounting firm. If you were an investor who uses financials to purchase companies, or even stocks, you would want, perhaps even demand, an independent audit of the company's books before you buy or invest. You wouldn't take the company's word that its financials were appropriately audited. The same holds true for companies, and especially for independent professionals that develop their own assessments and validate their own research data and then claim their instrument is validated. You must bear this distinction in mind when you compare the different assessments on the market and the various test providers. This chapter is about helping you understand what to ask and what to look for when selecting an assessment, as well as an assessment provider. I point this out because in my research there are, in fact, several test developers who have conducted their own validation studies in-house but have not had an independent review to critique and substantiate the results. As I have mentioned, one such third-party evaluator of assessments is the Buros Institute, publishers of the *Mental Measurements Yearbook*. An independent review board critiques and evaluates assessments in the marketplace and publishes its findings. If you cannot find the assessment you use on the Buros's website, there is a strong possibility the assessment has not been validated by this outside agency.

■ Reliability–Its Significance and Importance

While all assessments are validated to some degree, another measure of their utility is their reliability. This is often referred to as "test-retest reliability" and is just as important as validity. To be clear, *validated* means it accurately measures what it claims to measure and accurately predicts what it claims to predict. "Reliable" means it gives the same results today as it will next week or next month. A valid bathroom scale indicates how much you weigh; a reliable bathroom scale shows you weigh the same twice in a row. When we say that a scale or test cannot possibly be more valid than it is reliable, we mean that you can't say the scale got your weight right if thirty seconds later it showed a different weight.

As an example, the Myers-Briggs/MBTI, a very common, widely used assessment in measuring personality traits, comes up short on the test-retest reliability scale, placing only about half of all examinees in the same category (type) they were placed in the week before. Also, the Myers-Briggs is not validated as a selection tool because of its reliability, not its validity. This means that an instrument is valid in what it measures but its reliability may not give you the same results if you take it more than once. I have personally taken the MBTI. My results show me to be an INTP and then on another occasion show me to be an ENTP. Unless you are knowledgeable of the MBTI these symbols are meaningless to the average reader but what this means is it shows me to be two different people, one more extroverted and one more introverted. So which am I? The answer is I am both but the MBTI pigeon-holes me into who I was at the moment I took it. What is important to understand is that this is one of the reasons why assessments can be so confusing. The Myers-Briggs does not measure personality as deeply as necessary to justify its use as a selection or development tool.

The DiSC is another validated instrument, but it is not reliable enough to be used as a stand-alone selection tool, either. It has the same problem as the MBTI in the test-retest area. It's the reliability and the depth of what is measured, not its validity that is limiting its reach. This is a highly important distinction. The four-dimensional instruments like the MBTI, DiSC, Birkman, PI, and other popularized assessments may all have challenges in this area. I will discuss the four-dimensional model in more detail later in this chapter and its limitations in selection and development. As a point of reference, a well-designed assessment will yield a reliability factor of no less than .70 in its test-retest coefficient.

■ Beyond Validity and Reliability–What's Essential to Know?

Distortion, test construct, and test content are additional factors to consider. These features indicate what traits are and are not measured, as well as how deeply they are measured. Assessments are sold much like insurance products through distributors like DiSC and Profiles International, some are sold from franchise operators like Predictive Index, and some are sold direct like Caliper. Most practitioners or providers will only use or provide one assessment. You can't buy a Progressive Insurance policy from an Allstate or State Farm agent. Dealing with an independent insurance agency, you may be able to get multiple carriers. It is not likely someone would offer a Profiles XT and a Caliper together. I chose to remain independent and am in constant search of the best assessments on the market. I am always evaluating various assessments in an effort to keep abreast of what is on the market, what they measure, and how valid and reliable they are.

All assessments are validated to some degree and, while the question about validity and reliability are significant, there are other considerations that are also important. To help disseminate the simple from the sophisticated assessments, here are the questions you should ask to determine whether you're using a well-constructed instrument:

- How is the test designed and structured?

- How is distortion measured—whether a person is faking good or faking bad?

- How many distortion scales, if any, are used and what do they tell you?

- What is the test-retest coefficient reliability and consistency of the assessment over time?

- Is it forced choice or open choice?

- How long does it take to complete the assessment?

- How many and what kinds of behaviors and factors are measured?

- How deeply are the dimensions measured?

These are just some of the considerations and your provider should be able to help you evaluate whether you are using a quality assessment. If they can't, the odds are they don't know what they are providing you. The more sophisticated assessments usually meet these criteria while the simpler ones do not. Understanding what differentiates the various assessments and which ones will yield the greatest benefit is essential, and the payoff is well worth your time to evaluate what assessments to use.

■ What They Measure and the Depth of What They Measure

The process of using an assessment is, in fact, a way to measure someone, something, or some trait. When looking at an assessment, you need to ask yourself the following questions:

* What is it that I want to measure?

* How deeply do I want to measure what I'm looking to evaluate?

* What is the instrument of choice I will use? Ruler? Yard Stick? Tape Measure? Micrometer? Laser?

These questions need to be asked because not every assessment measures the same traits and not every assessment measures every trait. This is what I referred to earlier when I said it's what an assessment can't tell you that is important to understand. As an example, assessments like the PI, MBTI, DiSC, and Birkman are four-dimensional assessments; they measure four traits. The DiSC and the PI measure the same four traits. The Profiles XT measures nine behaviors and the 16PF Questionnaire measures sixteen. Some traits are measured with more depth than others. As an example, the Myers-Briggs, DiSC, and PI measure some but not all of the traits that are measured in the 16PF

Questionnaire, Hogan, or OPQ. The 16PF Questionnaire, Hogan, OPQ, and a few others are more sophisticated assessments and measure more traits than the MBTI, DiSC, and PI. What's even more significant is that they measure them at a deeper level than all the four-dimensional assessments. What I mean by measuring a trait deeper is that to weigh in on a certain personality trait, some assessments may have only three questions related to measure the trait and some assessments may have ten questions. Which do you think weighs in on the trait better? DiSC and PI don't have questions; they only use single words to describe behavior. This is why test construction is so important to understand when selecting an assessment. The Myers-Briggs assessment asks questions but only allows you to choose either/or answers, which pigeonholes the responses.

With the vast amount of assessments on the market, it is difficult to understand which ones to use as well as how to evaluate the results. Most of the time the assessment used by a company is the assessment most readily available, not the one most researched. Other reasons a particular assessment is used is because someone recommended it or it's easy to use and understand. The DiSC and the PI fall into this category, as they are very simple and easy to use but also very limiting. Unfortunately, people usually select the least expensive and or the simplest. However, selecting an assessment using this criteria is reducing the choice of an assessment to a commodity and means you're thinking of price, not substance or relevance, let alone validity and reliability. If a company does not use assessments as an integral part of its selection or development process then there will be less emphasis on the assessment process itself, which will lead to a shortage of valuable information about employees.

The assessments on the market are as different as the people they measure. There are simple assessments which include the four-dimensional assessments I have been referring to, and then there are those that are more sophisticated and are psychological in nature. The most important thing to understand is that the more sophisticated assessments measure behavior at a deeper and broader level and are more reliable. You get far more information when your assessment has the ability to evaluate the depth of an individual's behavior. The problem with the four-dimensional products on the market is they fall short in their reach and ability to do so, and their reliability is limited.

Four-Dimensional Assessments

The simple assessments I have been referring to are "four-dimensional," meaning they typically measure four behaviors: Dominance, Influencing, Steadiness, and Conscientiousness. The DiSC is indicative of this four-dimensional model. The PI/Predictive Index is also indicative of this model and uses the same four behaviors as the DiSC, but labels them differently. Predictive Index/ PI uses ABCD to define the same behaviors as the DiSC and they are interchangeable. Both instruments provide a three-graph model for visual representation to the degree to which a person exemplifies those traits. Both structure their assessments differently but they both ask you to select individual words that you feel define you and both assessments take about fifteen minutes to complete. These are examples of the simple instruments that measure general behavior traits. They are not sophisticated enough instruments to measure the depth of behavior to any significant level. I explain this in more detail in chapter 11 where I explore how behavior impacts leadership.

More sophisticated assessments are psychological assessments and require more training and expertise to interpret their meaning. The more sophisticated ones on the market are the 16PF Questionnaire and Hogan (both of which I use), and the OPQ, CPI, NEO, and a few others. These instruments require a higher level of understanding because they are more complex, and they usually take upward of forty minutes to complete because their questions (and results) are more extensive. Interpretation is more complex and more meaningful because you are using a stronger instrument that yields more information.

Most HR professionals have used some type of four-dimensional assessment. Unfortunately, the consistency of the results is a concern. I personally have ended up with different results from the tests. In the PI, for example, I am High A, High B, Low C, and cut back or mid-level D. The pattern from my PI is identical to my DiSC pattern. This should come as no surprise when you study the similarity of the two instruments. Then there is Profiles International and their product, the Profiles XT, which I have taken as well, and then the Birkman (using a four-color quadrant to demonstrate the four behaviors); there is also the Caliper and a host of others.

The four-dimensional assessments I have listed are inexpensive, simple to administer, simplistic by design, and easy to take (ten to fifteen minutes), and they give you a computer-generated report of the findings, often captured in what is referred to as a pattern. In the Myers-Briggs (MBTI) you might be an INTP or an ENTP or an ENTJ, which is how people are labeled. The MBTI is a good coaching tool but it has another drawback as there are certain traits it does not measure which limits its reach and effectiveness.

Besides these four-dimensional assessments, there are numerous others on the market as well, but typically they are what I call knockoffs of the versions I have mentioned. That is how Extended DiSC emerged. HR professionals are generally knowledgeable about most of the four-dimensional assessments and some are even certified in some of these instruments. All of these four-dimensional assessments have their value in certain applications but not in selection or development. They are better suited for team building, understanding the differences between employees, and helping to better understand the communication style in others.

In the vast majority of the reports generated from the four-dimensional assessments, you will find "soft" language. Essentially, this means it is difficult to tell if there are any problems or areas of concern because the results are always presented in such a favorable light. Given the results and the language in most reports, it is hard to discern whether a person has any underlying problematic or extreme behaviors. This is more problematic on the selection side than the development side. That's because on the selection side you will typically not have any prior data to draw from about an individual's behavior or performance. If the report you receive does not give you any red flags or areas of concern, how do you know if you are making a bad hire or a wrong promotion? If the assessment you are using does not provide the kind of results that provide insights into the kinds of behaviors you need to understand, it's likely you will make poor decisions on selection and promotion. To help you understand this concept, chapter 11 will get more into evaluating how behavior impacts performance and leadership.

If you take the DiSC assessment, your personality will be defined in similar terms as the MBTI in the form of a pattern. Taking an MBTI you will be labeled by a pattern, such as an INTP or an ENTP as I mentioned earlier. In the DiSC results you will be labeled by a pattern as well. Your pattern might identify you as a *Counselor* or *Perfectionist* or one of fourteen other patterns that the DiSC identifies. The PI does the same thing and uses sixteen patterns as well to describe people. The two tests just have different names for their patterns but, if you read the pattern descriptions, you will find they read almost identical. Another problem with this is that people become labeled by their pattern.

If you listen carefully to MBTI believers, they will tell you who they are by telling you what pattern they are.

"I am an ENTJ," they say, as if everybody knows what an ENTJ is. You will find the same thing with those who use the PI as you may be an *Altruistic* profile or the DiSC where you are a *Counselor* profile, as these kinds of assessments tend to label people. I use these examples to help state the case that these types of assessments are good for team building or understanding one another, as well as better understanding of why others do what they do. They are not designed to assess and evaluate leadership development or selection, nor are they strong enough to carry an assessment process that can support a world class leadership development program.

If you look at the PI and the DiSC training material, you would see they are extremely similar, if not identical in many ways. The DiSC material says you should not use the DiSC as a selection tool, but the PI touts theirs as a selection tool. I know the DiSC has the same challenges the MBTI does as it relates to reliability, and it is highly likely that every assessment on the market that uses a four-dimensional mode, including the PI, does as well. The construct of the DiSC and PI are different in that one is forced choice and the other is open choice. Both use a selection of individual words in their approach, but they construct them differently in the way you choose them. However, at the end of the day, they really aren't that different.

I have taken the Myers-Briggs, DiSC, PI, Profiles XT, and others just to see what they measure. I have been using the DiSC since 1991. While I am a certified distributor of the DiSC instrument, I know it is only acceptable to use in certain situations and I do not recommend it to my clients as a stand-alone selection tool, and especially not a leadership development tool. The DiSC has its place and is a great team-building tool. When used in a battery of assessments it can provide additional supporting data in evaluating behaviors, something you will see in chapter 12 on case studies. Understanding the different nuances of assessments will help you gain an understanding of what you are looking for and what to ask when you're looking for the right assessment and a practitioner to support you.

There are also specialty assessments like the Firo-B, the Murray Interests and the Holland Variables, and StrengthsFinder instruments that measure interest and motivation. These are unique instruments that can add to an individual's ability to gain more self-insight and can be part of the coaching equation, but they aren't revealing enough about a person's behavioral makeup. Another instrument somewhat different from many of the others is called the Profiles XT from Profiles International. It is a hybrid, meaning that it measures nine behaviors, incorporates the six Holland Variables, and has four cognitive scales. While it is a good instrument, it is lacking in a few areas. Most importantly, it lacks reach in the areas of workplace coping skills and emotional resilience; both significant factors that are identified by true psychological assessments and something I will explain more in-depth shortly. The Caliper, a very similar instrument to the Profiles XT, also falls short in the same way since it does not measure workplace coping skills.

Sophisticated Instruments

From my research some of the top instruments are the 16PF Questionnaire, Hogan, CPI, OPQ, and NEO. These are considered psychological in nature and provide deeper personality insights related to what is referred to in the world of psychology today as the "Big 5 Theory," which I will address in a moment. These assessments are more expensive and not readily available for general distribution because of the level of training needed to use and resell them. Of these five I use the 16PF Questionnaire and the Hogan, depending on the nature and needs of the situation. In chapter 12, "Case Studies," I will explain in detail the best uses for the 16PF Questionnaire and the Hogan. Both these tools can uncover behaviors that most assessments can't. In addition, I'll show how the Hogan brings confirming information to the results when used in our executive battery.

The 16PF 'Big 5' Theory and Psychology Today

Raymond Cattell, who developed the 16PF Questionnaire, was one of the early pioneers of personality testing. The following is taken from an article called "Big Five Personality Traits" and describes the relevance of the 16PF Questionnaire and its historical background which makes it one of the most reliable assessments on the market. This is from the article:[3]

---

[3] "Big Five Personality Traits," wikipedia.org. Retrieved from https://en.wikipedia.org/wiki/Big_Five_personality_traits on Nov. 30, 2015.

Early Trait Research

Sir Francis Galton in 1884 made the first major inquiry into a hypothesis that, by sampling language, it is possible to derive a comprehensive taxonomy of human personality traits. In 1936 Gordon Allport and S. Odbert put Sir Francis Galton's hypothesis into practice by extracting 4,504 adjectives which they believed were descriptive of observable and relatively permanent traits from the dictionaries at that time. In 1940 Raymond Cattell retained the adjectives, and eliminated synonyms to reduce the total to 171. He constructed a personality test for the clusters of personality traits he found from the adjectives, called Sixteen Personality Factor Questionnaire. Then, in 1961, Ernest Tupes and Raymond Christal found five recurring factors from this 16PF Questionnaire. The recurring five factors were: surgency, agreeableness, dependability, emotional stability, and culture. This work was replicated by Warren Norman, who also found that five major factors were sufficient to account for a large set of personality data. Norman named these factors surgency, agreeableness, conscientiousness, emotional stability, and culture; and these factors are through which the 5 Factor consensus has grown.

The 16PF Questionnaire is now in its fifth edition and has recently updated its norms.

The 16PF and the Big 5 Theory

The 16PF categories for the Big 5 model are: EX–Extraversion, ER–Emotional Resilience, TM–Tough-Minded, IN–Independence, SC–Self-Control. These are referred to as global factors. The global factors are then broken down further into subfactors that are referred to as primary factors to give deeper meaning to the trait. This is where the 16PF (Primary Factors) comes from. As an example the "D" of the DiSC and the correlating factor "A" of the PI both identify the level of dominance a person displays. The 16PF Questionnaire uses IN for the word "Independence" to define dominance as well. The difference is that the 16PF model breaks down the world of dominance into four subcomponents to help you see how the dominance is structured and what is underneath it. This is why this is a very detailed, in-depth assessment. More information on the use of these assessments will be found in chapter 11.

As I have discussed previously, I incorporate several different assessments in my practice, particularly when administering a battery of assessments for executive evaluation and development and, in so doing, the main instrument of choice is the 16PF Questionnaire. I have used it in nearly 13,000 evaluations over the last twenty-five years in the areas of selection and promotion, employee interventions, coaching, executive development, and succession planning. I have found it to be the single, most reliable and accurate assessment in predicting behavior and emotional resilience. It is one of the most, if not the most, sophisticated instrument on the market. Its value and accuracy has been proven countless times in my validation studies in a variety of different roles to include the world of leadership assessment. It has also consistently held up well across international borders from Asia to Europe to South America, and is available in more than thirty languages.

As I mentioned, another valuable tool I also incorporate into our assessment battery is the Hogan; I employ this when conducting our executive evaluations, executive coaching, and especially interventions. The Hogan has very similar characteristics to the 16PF Questionnaire. In fact, it complements the 16PF Questionnaire and provides a component called "derailers" that looks at how a person copes with challenges. However, there is one limitation with the Hogan. To get the same data I get from the 16PF Questionnaire in one report it requires two different reports from Hogan. Needing two reports from Hogan adds to the cost but, more importantly, the interpretation becomes more complex. Having to compare and contrast the two reports makes interpretation more challenging because you have to look at two different reports to interpret the meanings. Still, the Hogan is one of the better assessments on the market because it carries a high degree of validity and reliability and it is a great complement to our executive battery.

To show you the reach of the 16PF Questionnaire, we were chosen to conduct all of the leadership evaluations for the thirteen top executives in a $4 billion company located in the United States. Its parent company was located in Europe and the total global value of the organization was

$11 billion. We were chosen to evaluate and create development and coaching plans for the US executives and Dr. Steve O'Shaughnessy, a UK-based consultant, was chosen to do the same for the European executives. During a conference call to coordinate efforts on the project, I discovered that Dr. O'Shaughnessy also used the 16PF Questionnaire as well as the Hogan. I asked him why he used the 16PF Questionnaire in his practice and he said, "I believe the 16PF Questionnaire is a gold standard of psychometric testing." Who would have thought that two firms, thousands of miles away, asked to evaluate leadership traits around the world for an international company, would use the same instruments to measure behavior and create leadership development plans? Perhaps it speaks to the integrity and worldwide reach and universal acceptance of the 16PF Questionnaire and Hogan assessments.

Test Results–Integrity and Distortion
Understanding Faking Good and Faking Bad

When using any instrument, you need to know its true ability to predict personality. That's the validity and reliability piece I have been referencing. Beyond the validity and reliability of the assessment itself, there is the integrity of the assessment results of the individual who took the assessment. This is called *distortion*. The problem exists because not many assessments can discern distortion to any depth nor have a way to measure true distortion. Distortion is the degree to which an individual is faking good or faking bad. There is the validity and reliability of the assessment and then there is the validity and reliability of the results of someone's responses. These two results are entirely separate. You have to be able to measure distortion to see if the person is presenting himself in a different fashion from who he really is and be able to determine if the results of the assessment can be counted on as a fair representation of the individual who is taking the assessment. In other words, did he put on a different face when he took the assessment? This is why using more sophisticated assessments and especially multiple assessments is so valuable. A person might fool one assessment, but it is not likely that individual can fool a battery of assessments. This is yet another reason the 16PF Questionnaire is my instrument of choice because it has three distortion scales built into it.

■ Impression Management (IM) (24 weighted questions)

Impression Management, the first scale, is the tendency of the applicant to try to conform to societal expectations of making a good impression while taking the personality test. It is a person's slant on himself. It is normal for job applicants to try to look their best, especially in sales, so they will usually score above average on the Impression Management scale. Low scores may indicate self-esteem issues.

■ Infrequency (INF) (32 response indices)

The second scale, Infrequency, is based on the number of times the individual selected the "b" response or "?" alternative to one of the item stens (questions), for items on which most people readily make a decision. High scores on this scale correlate with indecisiveness, possible reading problems, concentration difficulties, or noncompliance, and may suggest a candidate is trying to hide something. In contrast, the MBTI, DiSC, PI and many others cannot measure Infrequency because of the way their assessments are constructed.

■ Acquiescence (ACQ) (103 true/false questions)

The third scale, Acquiescence, measures the person's tendency to agree, indiscriminately, with items on the test. High scores here may indicate disinterest in taking the assessment or may be related to comprehension or concentration problems.

As an example, while the 16PF Questionnaire has three distortion scales, the Profiles XT only has one. On this one particular distortion scale, the 16PF Questionnaire uses 103 True/False questions and the Profiles XT uses thirty-five yes/no questions. The three different distortion scales used by the 16PF Questionnaire make it superior in its ability to spot inconsistencies in a person's responses. While there are several thousand published articles on the 16PF Questionnaire, further evidence of its value is presented in Dr. Michael Karson's book, *16PF in Clinical Practice*, Dr. Jim Schuerger and Dr. Heather Cattell's book, *Essentials of 16PF Assessment* and Wendy Lord's two books *Personality in Practice* and *Overcoming Obstacles to Interpretation*. These authors are among the foremost authorities on the 16PF

Questionnaire. While I continue to explore the assessment landscape to search for the best instruments, my trust remains with the 16PF Questionnaire as one of the premier instruments that can support a quality selection model and a true leadership development model.

Workplace Coping Skills/Emotional Resilience

I stated earlier that an important distinction is what an assessment *can't* tell you. What this means is some assessments measure traits others don't. It's another important reason you need a more sophisticated instrument in measuring behavior and that is to capture a person's emotional resolve and coping skills. The 16PF Questionnaire is one of the more sophisticated instruments that can do this as it not only measures sixteen general dimensions of behavior, it also measures an individual's problem-solving ability as well. The four-dimensional assessments, and even the Profiles XT with its nine behaviors, does not reach deeply enough in measuring the emotional resolve of an individual. In our leadership work regarding high-potential executives, we know that there are eleven core traits in successful leaders that can be identified by the 16PF Questionnaire. In our case studies we can see when the 16PF Questionnaire has predicted the Peter Principle on numerous occasions.

Why Use a Battery of Assessments?

I have attempted to explain some of the differences in the various kinds of assessments and which ones to use. I have also explained why I have chosen the ones I use to help you understand what assessments will be most useful for your organization. My recommendation is that you use the 16PF Questionnaire and the Hogan because they are among the best on the market. Furthermore, I have also created a battery of assessments that include three behavioral/psychological assessments and three assessments related to measuring critical thinking and problem-solving skills. The combination of these six assessments is, in my view, the best all-around assessment model to help identify an executive's strengths and weaknesses. This assessment battery has an enormous predictive value and is useful for the selection, leadership development, and coaching models.

Selecting and Evaluating Your Provider

By now you should understand there are simple assessments (four-dimensional assessments) and more sophisticated assessments (psychological in nature and The Big 5 Theory), and why it is critical for you to understand the differences. However, there's more to evaluate than the assessment itself. During the entire assessment process, you must use a licensed practitioner who knows how to interpret the assessment, not just someone who sells you a report or recites what the report already tells you. The practitioner must be able to extract meaning from the report. The wrong assessment in the hands of an inexperienced practitioner will likely have a higher probability of failure, whether it's used for selection or development. Even the right assessment in the hands of an inexperienced practitioner is concerning. The following quote from Dr. Dave Watterson, another expert on the 16PF Questionnaire summed it up nicely. He explains just why it is so important to properly select the best assessment and the best provider or practitioner when he said:

> *"Merely buying a test doesn't necessarily guarantee you desired results. Just like a scalpel in the hands of a skilled surgeon, it is the surgeon not the scalpel that makes the difference. Looking at a particular test should not be the only criterion for its use. Looking at the process and whether you are working with a skilled practitioner who understands how to use the instruments is paramount."*

In Closing

Assessments are extremely complex leadership tools. Even the most experienced HR professionals can find them confusing because there is no uniform rating system covering all the assessments. There are some third-party evaluations but, still, choosing and using these tools remains challenging. Here are some closing thoughts.

Behavior is the biggest predictor of performance. In an effort to raise productivity and performance, a company can use assessments to improve their bottom line, reduce turnover, save on hiring costs, aid in succession planning, and help target leadership development. It is important to use the right assessment, particularly when you need to measure in-depth behavior and critical thinking skills. Currently, the four-dimensional assessments on the market are simply not deep enough to measure behavior and assess talent to the degree necessary.

Assessing real talent is best achieved through a battery of assessments that complement each other. A complete battery of assessments measures a person's behavior, emotional intelligence, how he manages himself when facing challenges as well as his critical thinking skills, problem-solving ability, and his intelligence. This type of application requires a more sophisticated set of assessments as well as an experienced practitioner who can gain the most insights from the information. By utilizing and incorporating more sophisticated assessments, along with the guidance of a skilled practitioner, an organization can optimize its ability to develop world class leaders and hire and retain the very best talent.

7

Three-Dimensional Leadership
Developing the Leader Within

A leader needs to focus on three main areas to create an effective, well-rounded development plan. Too often development plans only focus on a few areas the executive needs to work on but, in order to develop an executive to his or her fullest potential, the plans need to be comprehensive. There are many tools that can help people understand what is important, starting with the 360-degree assessment.

However, for whatever reason, too many individuals don't do anything to improve the areas highlighted in a performance review. It's a bit like when doctors tell their patients to quit smoking repeatedly and they keep smoking. Or obese individuals who lose weight and then put it back on. Many people are not willing to change whatever habits contributed to their medical or health issues. Similar behavior patterns exist in the workplace. Change is difficult because it requires a disciplined and concerted effort, a targeted focus, and a realistic plan. Just as people often need a support group or process to guide them in changing personal habits, they often need a similar arrangement for executive development.

Executives need help understanding how to develop themselves at a deeper level. They must utilize a disciplined approach and have a defined action plan for their professional development. To accomplish this, the program must include:

1. A corporate culture that supports and reinforces leadership development at all levels;

2. A set of expectations that people will be self-directed and self-disciplined in their learning and take ownership of their personal development;

3. A support system that helps the executives with their development; and

4. A way to identify the important areas for development and specific steps to effect change.

Having a personal trainer and a dietician, as well as a committed workout regimen will help someone lose weight and keep it off. Similarly, developing world class leaders requires a development program and support systems to help guide leaders through their development so ongoing change can take place.

This is so basic that it seems obvious that these steps would be followed but, in fact, it rarely happens to any significant level of effectiveness. In order for leadership development to gain any traction in an organization, a strong process and culture are required. There needs to be a model that helps the executive understand his or her strengths, weaknesses, and blind spots. This model will help the individual see what is needed to develop new skill sets, new job competencies, new behaviors, and new thinking skills. The end result is to help the executives create an action plan, with a set of actionable items that focuses on the strengths and weaknesses related to their leadership development.

The 3D Leadership Model ©

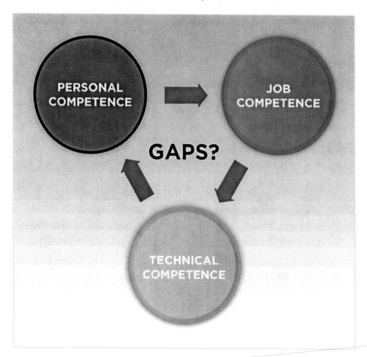

Figure 7.1 Three Essential Areas of Leadership Development

Leadership development needs to help the executive improve and develop in three distinct areas: new technical skill sets, new job competencies, and new behaviors. See Figure 7.1 on previous page. Each category must be identified and treated as a separate area of development because each one can derail an executive's performance and possibly a career. In analyzing these areas further, there are two key questions to ask:

1. What are the specific areas in which leadership development needs to take place for the executive?

2. How can we make sure that the executive is developing himself completely?

Capturing the extent of what someone must learn as it relates to a current role is as important as it is to prepare the person for future roles. To accomplish this it is important to understand that executive development is *not* just one-dimensional, it is three-dimensional. This is why I refer to it as my 3D Leadership Model. There are three core areas of development that must be addressed to create a well-rounded development plan:

1. Technical Competence (mastering hard skills)

2. Job Competence (mastering soft skills)

3. Personal Competence (mastering personal skills)

All three of these fields need to be evaluated and addressed separately when creating an executive development plan.

Equally important is matching the depth of the necessary development in each of these three topics to the level of the job.

■ Area 1 Technical Competence–Mastering the Hard Skills

This is the most obvious. This is about people needing to continue their education and field of study to help them advance in their careers. I will use accounting as an example of someone's technical skills, often referred to as hard skills. When people move up through an organization in accounting they may start out as a bookkeeper and then move to accountant, an accounting manager, then to a controller, then a CFO, and so on. They may begin with an associate's degree and then get a bachelor's degree in accounting, and then advance to a master's in business administration (MBA), or perhaps even get their certified public accountant's license (CPA). Beyond that they might commit to enrolling in advanced classes in economics, statistics, finance, or other related classes to give themselves stronger technical skills to support their accounting skills. All this study is part of an executive's continuous learning and development plan as it relates to accounting and expanding a depth of knowledge and technical expertise.

One young executive I was coaching had just finished his MBA in accounting. Even though he had a strong background in accounting and had continued his education in the accounting field, I asked if there was an area in which he still felt he was lacking and wanted to understand better based on his long-term career path. He commented that he wanted to learn more about cash flow analysis. We then discussed strategies to work with HR to put together a plan to improve that skill set. It was as simple as finding classes that focused on cash flow analysis and meeting regularly with the CFO to mentor him.

This scenario is applicable to engineering, manufacturing, human resources, or any other discipline. Continuing education around a person's technical skills is necessary. It becomes more critical as an individual is promoted within an organization. As the executive moves up in job levels and job titles, she takes on more responsibility as the roles become more complex. A lack of technical skills can become detrimental if the executive performs poorly, and can even be career ending. It goes without saying that enhancing these technical skills is one of the essential components in an executive's ongoing development.

■ Area 2 Job Competence—Mastering the Soft Skills

In any job, at any level, there are certain job competencies required that are not the same as an individual's technical skills and expertise. These are the intangible soft skills such as delegating, team building, conflict resolution, coaching, planning, organizing, and strategic planning, just to name a few. The lack of certain knowledge and experience will hinder a person's level of job competence. Preparing executives for what is to come can help them manage the new challenges they are going to experience. As a person advances in roles and responsibilities, job competencies become more and more critical and more complex.

In our talent management model, we have what we refer to as our Leadership Competency Inventory (LCI), which identifies thirty-eight different leadership competencies across eight major categories. There are many different resources on the market to help an organization establish specific competencies for different job levels. Without a focus and emphasis on developing these kinds of job competencies, it's only a matter of time before poor performance issues will surface. These competencies are learned skill sets that are developed over time; they are not usually innate competencies. In addition, there are other competencies that will be needed as an executive advances in his career.

Transition–The Unknown Competency

A competency that is often overlooked is what I call transition. I believe it is a critical element because transition is the constant evolution of what an executive goes though. It is as intangible as all the other soft skills. Transition is both a factual event and an emotional event. It's not the change that does people in, it's the transition. It's the emotional event that will create the most stress and impose the greatest challenges for the executive, and oftentimes they don't even realize its presence. The factual event is the new manager, the new location, the new job, the new corporate structure, the new reporting structure, the new company, and so on. These are more concrete and identifiable and can be rationalized and justified but that does not mean the executives accept them or have a buy-in.

The emotional event is that part of a person's transition that requires a change in mind-set and an acceptance of what is happening. The individual knows she is getting a new manager but doesn't accept this new situation. This is when an executive needs to change her thinking. One example of transition is when a person advances from an individual contributor role to a role where she is managing others. From the role of managing others, she then moves to a role of managing managers, and so on.

There is a major difference between roles in a domestic position versus an international role, as the latter is likely to be more dynamic and is a more complex assignment. The point is that each new role will create another transition and set up an emotional state that the executive will go through. Each time someone moves into a new role with new responsibilities, the person's learning resets back to zero. The new role will create a set of circumstances the employee has never experienced before. As an example, when a young executive is first promoted, he must learn to transition from doing things by himself to getting things done through others, not telling others what to do.

The degree of challenges that results in a person's transition can be career ending if not developed and managed properly. Moving from being an individual contributor to someone who manages others requires new competencies, new behaviors, and new thinking. Later, when someone moves from managing others to managing managers it requires yet another set of competencies. More importantly, a new way of thinking must emerge. This transition could be anything from moving from an individual contributor role to changing business units or companies, to managing the differences in cultures, managing others, managing managers, working cross-culturally, and working internationally.

Transition Applied to Practice

Here is an example of transition and being able to understand what you are doing and being able to see your impact. One of the individuals I coached was in a new role as plant manager running a manufacturing company. He was so excited about making changes that he overwhelmed the organization; he created pockets of resistance because he did not understand his own transition, let alone his staff's resistance to his changes. He failed to understand the simple leadership and team-building competency and the philosophy that says, "People support what they help create." Instead, he created resistance by his top-down style and failed to get buy-in along the way.

In another example, a service manager was promoted to branch manager. He believed the branch lacked structure and discipline. Immediately upon becoming manager, he put things in place—the things he felt were lacking. He put in his idea of structure and discipline, to the detriment of staff morale, and within a year a union organizing took place. He became the enforcer of rules, which is not a quality of a good leader. It's obvious this person did not manage the transition into his new role at all. While there are other factors at play, the manager was unable to understand and manage the transition as well as understand the competencies, behaviors, and new thinking skills that he really needed in his new role. Now imagine the same thing happening in a larger role, such as when a person takes over a major department or division, or even a company. The downside risk can have huge repercussions and, unfortunately, continues to happen throughout corporate America.

Strategic Competencies

Besides understanding the impact of transition, you shouldn't underestimate or ignore the other intangible competencies (soft skills) like managing the strategic aspects of the job. Here is where more strategic competencies, such as realigning duties, facilitating a turnaround, improving productivity, and creating a strategic plan, as well as taking on complex and new activities and duties, are required.

Special Situations

There are special situations and responsibilities when working cross-culturally, dealing with the Gen X and Gen Y dynamics, women in a male-oriented environment, diversity, getting an international assignment, and so on, that need to be managed and understood.

Business Acumen as a Competency

Another circumstance that surfaces in the area of competencies is when an executive moves up in roles and responsibilities that require a strong degree of business acumen. This encompasses all the fiduciary responsibilities of making prudent decisions, understanding how business works, having industry knowledge, and being customer focused. Additional business acumen competencies include launching a product, opening up a new facility, managing a turnaround, managing mergers and acquisitions, taking a company public or private, and even managing a global landscape. These are all additional responsibilities executives will face at some point and will need to be prepared to handle when they arise.

For evidence of how some individuals faltered and failed to master some of these competencies, refer back to chapter 1, where I discussed CEOs from various companies, including Coca-Cola, Mattel, Enron, and American Apparel, whose CEO was, in fact, fired twice. Where were their gaps? What situations did they not anticipate? Could these CEOs have overcome them with better preparation? With the proper leadership development plan and process in place, could their careers have been salvaged?

An Example of Complexity

Here is an example that encompasses new competencies, transition, strategic aspects, business acumen, special situations, and new assignments. I was interviewing one of several internal candidates who were being considered to manage the overseas operations of a client. I asked him if he was fully prepared to move overseas tomorrow and take over operations. He immediately and confidently responded, "Yes, I am very confident." Then, I asked him, "How much time have you spent understanding the cultural and political differences you will be faced with as you take over the responsibility of growing the international operations?"

As he pondered my question, he realized this was an area he was not prepared for and had not even considered. The message is, "you don't know what you don't know." Without any preparation or acknowledgement that this needs to be part of his focus, it is likely that he will have a difficult time because not only had he not thought of it, it is not a competency he had ever planned or prepared for. Much like shortcomings in technical skills, the lack of job competencies can create performance issues as well. This statement I made earlier is worth repeating here: *Upon promotion into management one becomes mystically endowed with all the traits necessary to hire and create a staff that gets the job done.*

No one comes equipped with all the traits necessary to hire and manage a capable staff. Ironically, somehow this concept seems to escape us when we hire and promote people. Even more concerning is that the people we hire or promote into these new roles usually don't see it coming, either. Their egos and prior successes blind them to the reality of the new position.

You may have witnessed some of these difficulties yourself. You may have also seen, as I have, great salespeople who were promoted to a sales management role and then failed in that role. You may have seen great engineers promoted to engineering managers and then fail in that new role. These kinds of failed promotions happen all the time. However, they can be prevented if there is a better process in place to evaluate an individual's capabilities. Some people are simply not prepared for the roles and assignments they receive. Companies should help employees prepare for their new positions and, even more importantly, shouldn't put the wrong people in the wrong positions. Unfortunately, it happens far more than it should.

At one point in my career, I decided to further develop the competency of strategic planning as a personal initiative. I challenged myself to further develop my own business acumen skills in this area. By the age of thirty, I had owned and sold three companies. Then, I spent the next decade in corporate America, including an international role and involvement in two acquisitions along the way. Having been involved in four acquisitions in my career, I assumed I was fairly adept at strategic planning, M&A, and turnarounds. One of the reasons I felt that way was because in my first corporate role, just after I sold my businesses, I engineered a turnaround of an underperforming division. In the acquisition that I led, things turned out well but, in hindsight, I know that I could have handled it better. I encountered situations that I hadn't dealt with earlier. There are lessons that come from our past businesses experiences. As time went on I came to realize I was overstating my capabilities and had an overly aggressive view of my talents. I probably had more to learn, even in what I considered my area of expertise.

At the age of forty-two, I came across a book on strategy called *Strategic Planning, What Every Manager Must Know* that opened my eyes to things I had not even thought of and, over the course of the next year, I read seven different books on strategic planning, two books on mergers and acquisitions, and two books on managing turnarounds. What I absorbed from these books was eye-opening, to say the least. Managing a turnaround, strategic planning, and M&A are three different competencies that are essential aspects of business acumen. None of them are easy to understand, let alone master. You simply can't lump them together since they all encompass different skill sets. I realized that learning is never ending and you really don't know what you don't know. I share my personal experience with you to emphasize we all have egos and we all have beliefs that get in our way of learning new things. Having a preconceived notion that we know it all has led to the downfall of some of the most successful leaders. Here are some examples of past leaders whose belief system and perhaps even their position got in their way of their thinking and judgement.

"Everything that can be invented has been invented."
—Charles H. Duell, Director of US Patents, 1899

*"There is no likelihood man can ever
tap the power of the atom."*
—Robert Millikan, Nobel Prize in Physics, 1923

"I think there is a world market for about five computers."
—Thomas J. Watson, Chairman, IBM, 1943

*"There is no reason for any individual to
have a computer in their home."*
—Ken Olsen, President, Digital Equipment Corporation, 1977

The comments from these executives in key leadership and influential positions were blinded by their own success. As leaders they somehow failed to understand what they did not know.

Developing and preparing new leaders to lead is essential and can only be done by having a world class leadership development program that focuses on the gaps and areas of development. There must be a set of competencies defined to help executives recognize they have a greater chance of success if they commit to learning on an ongoing basis. To that end, a competency model is extremely necessary to help guide the executive in their development in this area.

■ Area 3 Personal Competence–Mastering Self-Insight

Developing the leader within you requires you to learn to *lead from within*. Leading from within is harder than you might think because it requires a level of self-insight and self-awareness, enabling you to truly understand yourself before you can be an effective leader. It means you have to be willing to look and search deep within yourself to understand your own gaps. Leo Tolstoy, the Russian novelist, was ahead of his time when he said, "Everyone thinks of changing the world, but no one thinks of changing himself." Many executives can't accept they need to change their inner world before they can interact more effectively with others in the workplace.

In the world of psychology and the study of human behavior, especially behavior in the workplace, it has been shown that behavior is the single biggest predictor of performance. An executive needs to understand how his personality, behavior, and thinking style can affect his success and possibly derail his career. It's not only the executive's lack of self-insight; it's often his unwillingness to address the issues. A common reason for performance improvement plans (PIPs) and termination is a person's behavior. Issues become evident from people's attitude, demeanor, approach, etc. Mastering personal competence and making behavioral changes is difficult for almost everyone.

Self-insight and self-management are essential developmental areas. Consider the difference between someone who is full of himself because he sees himself as smarter than other people and needs to see how innocent celebrations might make others see him as egotistical, versus someone who *is* egotistical and needs to be reminded of his imperfections. In the world of leadership, there is a gentle balance between getting ahead and getting along.

Highly dominant and competitive individuals who need to be in control and in charge are prone to getting into power struggles and conflict with others. Unfortunately, some leaders never quite figure out how to balance the work of getting ahead and getting along.

What I am referring to is the level of an individual's self-insight and self-awareness and his ability to manage himself. It is related to a person's level of self-control as well as his level of emotional intelligence. As an example, think about someone's faulty belief that he can handle his liquor well while on a business outing. Can he recognize the difference between social drinking while just out with colleagues or being at a business meeting or a corporate function, and overindulging or even binge drinking? It's knowing when to quit and knowing when you're making a fool of yourself. This is the essence of emotional intelligence, self-insight, and self-control.

Another example of self-insight and self-awareness occurs when you're talking to people. Can you recognize when you're talking over people instead of listening to them? Can you recognize when you're speaking and listening or when you're talking down to them? This is a major distinction that cannot be overlooked when communicating with others. It's knowing the difference between speaking from judgment versus observation, and its impact, or the difference between criticizing someone and critiquing someone. These behaviors are reflected in the competencies we refer to as communication and listening skills. A person's behavior and thinking style impact his ability to manage personal competence, and most executives would be well served to make improvements in this area. In the medical field it is referred to as "bedside manner." The concept of thinking before you speak, or the old cliché, "watch your tongue," are certainly evidence of a person's demeanor and personality.

■ Behavior–Its Impact on the Job and Performance

Here is an example of how personality and thinking style can impact a person's job competence and the decisions the individual will make around their role. Let's say we own a business and we decide we want to hire a risk manager. The person who applies has a PhD in statistics and analytics from Harvard. You'd say those are impressive credentials! Let's also say this person likes to deal only with the facts, just the facts. Some of you may remember there was a character in the old TV series *Dragnet* named Sergeant Joe Friday, whose character epitomized this personality. For those of you who never saw Joe in character, suffice it to say, Sergeant Joe Friday was very no-nonsense, very serious, and wanted just the facts. As he would question his witnesses and suspects and go about obtaining information he would say, "Just the facts, nothing but the facts."

Other behaviors our applicant has besides being fact based is that he is data driven, while possessing a cautious, conservative, and risk-averse approach to his work. He hates to be wrong, often overanalyzes everything, and worries about failing and making poor decisions. Now, if the open position is to mitigate any and all risk, this candidate might be the right person to hire. However, this person, as smart as he is, will have difficulty in the role because his behavior and his thinking are likely to create challenges. His personality, by its very nature, is risk averse and he is likely to stymie business growth because of his conservative, cautious nature. Yet his credentials—having a PhD in statistics and analytics from Harvard—will likely get him the role.

On the opposite side, we have another candidate who applies for the same position; he has a PhD in statistics and analytics from Yale. This person has an entirely different set of behaviors. He is the eternal optimist, does nothing in moderation, and believes you can't make egg salad without breaking some eggs. You win some and you lose some, so let your winners run. Learn to cut your losses short since you cannot win every time and you just have to manage the risk. If this person has a gambler mentality and is impulsive, he may go overboard in his decisions and cost the company a lot of money with a free-wheeling mentality. These are two very different people with two very different styles and different sets of behaviors. I have repeatedly stated that behavior *is* the single biggest predictor of performance, and you can see in these two extreme examples how this happens.

Personal competence is a person's DNA or hardwiring. There is a saying, "The eye cannot see the eye." It refers to a person's inability to see himself as he truly is. Can a gymnast critique his or her routine in the middle of the routine? Of course not. For the same reasons, neither can an executive critique his personal competence when he's busy in the trenches. He may be blinded by his personality traits and thinking style. Or he may be blinded by his past successes or by a big ego. This type of person may believe he doesn't need help or advice. When an executive's ego outweighs his abilities, cannot see his own flaws, cannot admit he needs help, and cannot recognize that he's in over his head, the end result is often fatal. And as in the case of Jeffrey Skilling at Enron it may not just be only the person's career, but the organization as well.

Ego by itself, if not kept in check, can be a major problem. Think of the great skiers who jump off helicopters to ski in the backcountry and lose their lives to an avalanche. Think of the great mountain climbers who have died at the summit or the rock climbers who took one too many chances. These great athletes, with incredible skills, experience, and talents, lose their lives because of overconfidence and, ultimately, they make poor choices. Unfortunately for them, the choices are life ending. In the business world, poor choices can be career ending.

When a leader lacks personal competence the wrong behaviors are likely to emerge. This is evident when someone makes destructive comments, needs to be right, needs to have everything perfect, needs to be the smartest person in the room, micromanages, and is controlling. These are some of the behaviors that can put other people off and derail an executive. This is why using assessments to evaluate a person's makeup, creating an internal feedback loop and executive coaching are so essential.

There are two aspects to personal competence: how we manage ourselves and how we manage our behavior in regard to our relationships with others. Learning what the attributes are as they relate to each area is critical to professional presence and the ability to master personal competence. Learning to master this will go a long way in helping executives succeed at higher and higher levels.

In Closing

Three-Dimensional leadership is absolutely essential in developing world class leaders. To put people in the right roles and provide them with the tools they need to grow and develop, two steps must occur. One is evaluating their true ability to handle the roles and responsibilities they are being considered for. This is where a more sophisticated battery of assessments can provide valuable insight. The second is to do a gap analysis in order to identify the developmental needs across all three areas in the 3D Leadership model. Then, an organization must assemble and support an effective developmental plan to help the executive move through the steps and encourage their progress. By following these critical steps, you can help ensure you are preparing your leaders for success.

CHAPTER

8

Strategic Leadership Assessment
Establishing the Feedback Process and an Accountability Model

In the previous chapter I examined the three essential components that need to be part of any executive's leadership development plan. This chapter will focus on what is needed to provide the crucial feedback to the executive. It is important to have a process that uncovers all of an executive's strengths and weaknesses so that the real parts of development can be identified. There needs to be a culture within the process that supports leadership development and a built-in accountability model that sets expectations. Here are the mechanisms that need to be in place to help assure a successful outcome:

* a process that creates a robust accounting of strengths and weaknesses across all three of the areas of leadership development

* a way to provide critical feedback that is meaningful

- specific action plans to follow that show a clear path to success

- a set of expectations and defined goal or goals

- a methodology to hold the executive accountable

To accomplish all of this, it is essential the executive receives feedback from all three sections related to leadership development. To do this effectively, information must come from several sources, not just one. For instance, using a 360-degree assessment to help an executive bring about change or only using an executive coach is not sufficient; neither is using a single assessment. Using one or the other won't provide enough insight into all the issues that need to be evaluated. For development to be effective we must think in terms of the total resources available to help leaders gain insight into their gaps to enable them to reach their fullest potential. I refer to this as "Strategic Leadership Assessment." In chapter 5, "Creating an Internal Feedback Loop," I explained the importance of leaders receiving feedback from multiple sources to give them multiple perspectives. Strategic Leadership Assessment has to be more than just a Key Performance Indicator on an executive's list of things to do.

Strategic Leadership Assessment–The Process

"Strategic Leadership Assessment" is the process of gaining insight into an individual's makeup and identifying what his true strengths and weaknesses are across all three areas of leadership, as described in the 3D Leadership model. It consists of a series of events designed to identify and capture all of the significant information about an executive.

There needs to be a way to identify those people in the organization who are considered to have the potential to advance higher in the organization. This process is the basis for doing just that while, at the same time, filling the leadership pipeline. Using this process helps set the stage to evaluate the existing talent to determine who is a viable choice for the high-potential group and where they might be slotted to support the succession planning process. If any of the components or steps are omitted, the process and the executive may be derailed. Here are the components that need to evolve in order to accomplish the desired outcome:

■ STEP 1: MANAGEMENT INTERVIEW

The first step is to conduct an in-depth interview with the manager. By conducting this interview, you will get a complete overview and historical perspective of the individual, his role, his successes and failures, and any potential concerns or future expectations. The interview should cover three distinct elements.

Part 1: Job Identification

The management interview should consist of a review of the job description and its requirements, what is expected in the role, and the challenges currently affecting the role. This is where understanding the gaps and problems the individual is experiencing in the role is critical. On one coaching assignment, I asked the reporting manager to walk me through the entire facility and show me the areas of responsibility that a particular executive was responsible for from the warehouse, including the kinds and complexity of the products assembled, and the various manufacturing lines. It was important to understand the size, complexity, and the extent of the role to help me determine where the issues the executive was having were coming from. Was it a lack of technical skills, a lack of certain job competencies, or were behaviors and critical thinking skills impacting his performance? The possibility existed it was in all three areas but, until all the information was obtained by asking questions and conducting the appropriate assessments, it would be hard to pinpoint where the problem was coming from.

In a more complex and dynamic situation, I was brought in to conduct an intervention. The executive was the vice president of international operations who oversaw manufacturing of foreign operations and lost $1.1 million in the first fourteen months in the role. Coming from one of the Big 3 firms, this individual was responsible for managing two plants, twenty miles apart, operating 24/7 with 2,800 people. This person supervised 60 percent of worldwide production of a $2 billion tier-one supplier to the auto and truck industry. The need to understand the requirements and complexity of a role is directly related to the executive's ability and potential development plan. In this case there was relevance to the size and complexity of the role but that was not the only thing impacting this individual's poor performance. This situation will be explored further in chapter 12, "Case Studies."

Part 2: Performance Reviews

During the management interview it is also important to review any and all prior performance reviews to obtain a greater insight into the person's past and present performance. This may not be as revealing or as helpful as desired because many performance appraisals don't reflect the individual's performance for various reasons. It is not uncommon to find people who have not had a review in several years. It's important to take into consideration what has or hasn't been addressed with the executive that may provide insight to support the process. Depending on the size of an organization, the president, human resource manager, and the reporting manager may handle the performance reviews. Evaluating past performance reviews will send a clearer message to the individual regarding the significance of the situation. This process will help everyone involved get clearer pictures of the issues surrounding the executive and his desired outcome. Most importantly, the executive will have better insight into the help that may be needed. If there is an executive coach assigned, the coach will have better insight into the assignment and clarity about the individual being coached.

Part 3: Clarify Objectives

In the beginning of any development plan, it is important to clearly define the goals and objectives so everyone knows what is expected, what the issues are, and what the outcome is expected to be. All parties should be included so that the mission, expectations, and assignments are understood. This is a critical area to address but we often soft pedal or down-play any negative issues or concerns because we don't want to hurt anybody's feelings, or upset a valued executive because we can't afford to lose him. However, regardless of the reason, not being upfront in the first place undermines the process and is a recipe for disaster. To undervalue and underestimate this initial piece is a mistake. At the outset, there must be a discussion of whether the objective for leadership development is based on a performance issue, a need for development to help the manager in the current role, or to prepare the person for advancement and what he will need for his next role. Clarifying the objective is critical. It sets the tone for the engagement. Doing this due diligence up front pays big dividends and gets the process off to a good start; otherwise, the process is doomed.

■ STEP 2: EXECUTIVE ASSESSMENT

Step two involves assessing the individual with a thorough process. As critical as the management interview is, conducting a thorough executive assessment is just as important. This part consists of four different components that are designed to help an executive gain self-insight, understand strengths and weaknesses, and identify any gaps. This series of activities is designed to uncover more information, beyond what was disclosed in the management interview.

Part 1: Leadership and Life History Brief

Using the Leadership and Life History Brief, the executive documents his background, work history, philosophy and beliefs, successes and failures. I do this by having the executive fill out our *Leadership and Life History Brief,* which is a document we designed to chronicle much of an executive's career, along with detailing how the individual views his own successes and failures. They are asked to evaluate and rate themselves across nine leadership competencies.

It is important to understand how perfect they see themselves. This could be done by conducting an interview, but I prefer to give a written assignment. This way the individual has time to reflect on what he has done, where he has been successful, what he has learned, where he is presently in his career, and what potential obstacles are in his way. This exercise helps to see how people see themselves through their own lens and how honest and accurately they are assessing themselves. It gives them a baseline to launch their development.

Part 2: Assessments

In chapter 6, "Exploring the World of Assessments," I wrote about the differences between a simple and a sophisticated assessment and introduced the concept of incorporating a battery of assessments. This part of the evaluation is where a battery of assessments is essential to help measure the depth of an individual's behavioral makeup and problem-solving ability. To use a Myers-Briggs, DiSC, PI, Birkman, or any other four-dimensional assessment is not sufficient for this exercise. A full range of assessments must include behavior, personality, reasoning and problem-solving skills to assess true fit and developmental areas.

In our executive battery we utilize six different assessments that measure personality, emotional resolve, and how people respond to stress. Within the battery there are also a series of critical thinking skills assessments that measure learning agility, inductive and deductive reasoning, and perceptual reasoning. Perceptual reasoning is commonly referred to as a person's natural problem-solving ability or IQ. Utilizing these six assessments and what they can reveal about an executive's capability and potential, not only helps the executive gain additional perspective, but the organization can utilize the information to help establish the individual's potential to fill the leadership pipeline and support the succession planning objectives. This is part of the process needed to identify high-potential individuals.

Part 3: 360-degree Assessment

The 360-degree assessment will address leadership competencies in different areas and reveal how others perceive the same competencies, and whether there are any disconnects between how the individuals sees themselves, how their managers sees them, and how others see them.

The 360-degree assessment we use evaluates thirty-two competencies. There is value in utilizing a 360 because the results bring in the perspective of other members of the organization. Often, they are consistent with the rest of the data that comes from other parts of the process and, oftentimes, new and valuable pieces of information are revealed. At their worst they are less then revealing for reasons previously discussed.

In chapter 5, "Creating an Internal Feedback Loop," I discussed the pros and cons of the 360. Sometimes, the 360 does provide the depth of information you need, but doesn't yield the results you need to help have an impact on the process. Still, they are helpful, but you need to have a set of leadership competencies and provide a way for honest feedback and comments. More importantly, you need a process that helps assure meaningful results. If you are going to use a 360 in the evaluation process you need to commit to conduct another one in eight to ten months to see if any progress has been made.

There must be a commitment to doing another 360 in a way that focuses on results and outcomes, and reassessing accomplishments. Otherwise, my recommendation is that you shouldn't waste the time, money, and effort. If the executive knows that another 360 will be conducted at a future date, he may take the whole process more seriously and realize that if he doesn't make any changes, it will be very obvious. This is one way in which you begin to establish an accountability focus.

Part 4: Interviews with Peers and Key Stakeholders

In-depth interviews are essential, not just with the reporting manager but any senior manager, peer, or key stakeholders within the organization who have a vested interest in the success of the engagement. This can help provide insight into the specific issues and dynamics. These may be individuals who are participants in the 360 as well as other stakeholders who were not included in the original 360 but who have significant input to contribute to the process.

Individual interviews are conducted with peers and subordinates and any essential stakeholders to get a clear picture of how effectively the executive manages their role and interacts with others. My experience has proven that, more often than not, the interview process reveals more valuable information than the 360 itself. This is because people are more comfortable talking to an unbiased third party than putting their thoughts in writing about someone. This can be done internally within the organization; however, when a third party conducts this part of the process people are more willing to discuss the issues in confidence. This is especially true when an individual is afraid to say what really needs to be said, fearing retribution or retaliation. When this happens, the entire initiative can be sabotaged if the critical issues never get addressed and brought out in the open.

■ STEP 3: GAP ANALYSES

The purpose of the gap analysis is to evaluate all the information gathered in steps 1 and 2. We compare and contrast all this information with the assessment component to do a gap analysis. Table 8.1 shows all of the information that will be assimilated to perform the gap analysis.

Management Interview	Executive Assessment
Job Identification	Leadership and Life History Brief
Performance Reviews	Executive Battery - Personality and Problem-Solving Assessments
Clarify Objectives	360-Degree Assessments
	Peer Interviews with Stakeholders

Table 8.1 Components of a Gap Analysis

The gap analysis is a critical part of the process and should not be omitted for several reasons. This information almost always correlates to the performance issue or gap. It often supports the information that comes from the other areas. When an executive receives all this feedback from multiple perspectives it becomes easier to open a dialogue of meaningful purpose that opens up the lines of communication and reduces the defensive posture of the executive. In essence, it is harder for the individual to hide and deny the facts. Greater acceptance is often the outcome as the obvious usually emerges. Conducting an in-depth analysis of the findings can reveal not only where the gaps are but where the strengths are as well. Conducting a gap analysis is the most important thing you can do, but it is impossible to conduct an in-depth gap analysis until you do all the preliminary evaluations.

You cannot build a solid development plan until you conduct a thorough gap analysis. Conducting a thorough gap analysis brings in all the information to help identify the executive's real strengths and weaknesses. The gap analysis takes into consideration job-related issues, competency-related issues, and behavior issues as described earlier in the chapter. The gap analysis also takes into consideration performance reviews, 360-degree assessment data, peer reviews, and assessment data. With all this information at hand, the obvious begins to emerge as it relates to creating a development plan. The information generated about an executive from the gap analysis helps identify the true potential of the individual. This depth of information is also a source used to identify people to fill the high potential pool and, ultimately, fill the leadership pipeline. The entire process provides a way to identify those individuals who may be considered capable of filling the succession planning process.

■ STEP 4: EXECUTIVE DEBRIEF AND FEEDBACK

When all this information is compiled, it is time to debrief the executive and provide them the feedback from their results. By utilizing all of the feedback from all of the different resources, the executive can then work through all of the data and determine what the key takeaways are from what has been presented. Using these resources the executive will be able to create a unique development plan that he fully owns.

■ STEP 5: STRATEGIC LEADERSHIP DEVELOPMENT PLAN

Once the feedback and debrief is completed, and the executive has received all the information from the feedback sessions and the results of the gap analysis, he will begin to construct his own development plan complete with goals and timelines. It is not likely that a manager is equipped to coach someone when all these things are factored in. Therefore, either a qualified individual within the organization can be engaged as a coach or, in some cases, an external executive coach needs to be brought in. The following action items will serve as a road map as the executive begins to break down this information into the three areas of development and formulate a development plan.

Part 1: Identify Strengths, Weaknesses, Opportunities, and Threats (SWOT)

The executive conducts his own personal SWOT analysis after all of the information is presented. He will evaluate his past performance reviews, assessment data, peer and stakeholder interviews, and 360 reviews to determine where he needs to improve. By looking through the data presented, hopefully the executive can have an honest assessment about what the information reveals and then can identify where and how to make improvements.

Part 2: Plan Objectives and High-Payoff Activities

Next, the executive maps out a plan and identifies his top six high-payoff activities. From those high-payoff activities, he further defines the key one or two issues to begin to work on. It is difficult for someone to work on any more than one or two issues at a time, on top of all of the other job responsibilities, not to mention any outside interests such as family, recreation, or continuing education. From these high-payoff activities the executive will begin to map out the specific action items to move their initiatives forward.

Part 3: Specific Resources and Strategies

Identifying the appropriate resources, whether that is internal or external to the organization, is the next step in the process. The company may choose to use an internal or external coach. A good option is to hire a coach for one-on-one coaching sessions over a six-month timeframe to help focus on the developmental plan. A coach adds value to the process by assisting with the practice of specific skills, providing a sounding board, and keeping the process on track. A coach also adds an element of accountability as the coaching engagement requires a commitment in time and energy. Strategies may also include going back to college, identifying opportunities through specific courses at local universities or community colleges, and attending classes or workshops of interest. They may identify specific articles, books, and topics to read in order to gain further insight into areas in which the executive wants to improve. These initiatives should be spread across all three of the areas of development related to technical competence, job competence, and personal competence that have been addressed. Only focusing on one area limits an individual's growth and defeats the purpose of the developmental initiative.

Part 4: Identify with Stakeholders

It is important for the executive to identify any other people inside or outside the organization who may be influential and instrumental to help him work through specific challenges or issues. Identifying the stakeholders who can provide necessary feedback and insight as well as provide opportunities for professional discussion can encourage the executive to work through any specific challenging areas. It is another important area in which an executive can get feedback and support along the way.

Part 5: Make a Timeline

Creating a specific timeline will put emphasis on immediate results in a timely manner. It helps to create and sustain momentum and ward off procrastination before it gets out of hand. In addition, knowing that the process will be repeated again in eight to ten months will most likely prompt the executive to immediately start the development process, hopefully gaining immediate traction.

Part 6: Network for Support

Being transparent and comfortable reaching out to others who may provide a supportive network will be critical so that the executive does not feel he is going it alone. Often having a sounding board with whom to confide and receive honest objective feedback can be encouraging and helpful.

Part 7: Be Able to Give Evidence of Support

Show small wins! Small wins lead to bigger wins and being able to show success brings with it a sense of accomplishment. You may be familiar with the TV show *The Biggest Loser.* The show is all about a team effort where everyone is supporting one another to lose significant amounts of weight and each week has a weigh-in. The same holds true for development; there needs to be support to help individuals achieve specific milestones to show success and celebrate progress.

Part 8: Review Progress with Shareholders

Shareholders play an important role. Searching for feedback from those supporters and people who have provided the executive insight into areas of development can be critical along the way to ensure and reinforce that progress is being made.

■ STEP 6: REVIEW AND EVALUATE RESULTS IN EIGHT TO TEN MONTHS

It is important to measure the progress of the executive and what has been accomplished. This requires a follow-up 360-degree assessment somewhere down the road. It may even be beneficial to conduct peer interviews as well. It is important to assess the progress of the executive as it relates to his development plan. This reinforces the expectations that their professional development is something to be taken seriously. It also allows others a voice as to whether they see improvement and changes in the individual. It further reinforces the organization's emphasis on continuous learning and supports a policy that leadership development is part of an ongoing process where measurable, sustainable results are expected. The follow-up process in eight to ten months reinforces the fact that the executive is accountable for their results and needs to do something with the information and the exercise as part of the evaluation.

In Closing

This chapter has created a process and a track for the executive to run on for growth and development. Perhaps most important is creating an accountability process. As mentioned earlier, it is not uncommon for people to start something, lose momentum and then not finish. There are many people who go to college, then quit and never finish. There are many people who go on diets, lose some weight, but put the weight right back on. Likewise, there are many executives who over time derail their careers and lose their jobs because they fail to commit to their own professional development. The Strategic Leadership Assessment program helps the feedback process create an accountability model. This is part of having a world class leadership development program that promotes and develops world class leaders.

CHAPTER

9

The Value and Process of Executive Coaching

One of the most valuable activities an organization can do to create a world class leadership development program is to invest in its staff. Providing resources such as executive coaching is not only critical to the success of the organization and the significance of the leadership development program, but can ultimately lead to the success–or failure–of an executive. It stands to reason then that one of the components necessary in a leadership development program is the use of an executive coach. However, getting the appropriately trained coach is not as simple as you might think.

In order for the coaching initiative to reach a successful outcome, the organization must commit to creating an internal culture that embraces coaching, and this mindset must be driven from the top. It must be evident to all employees that the CEO and upper management expect the initiatives to be taken in regards to self-improvement, leadership development, and executive coaching.

Creating a Coaching Culture and a Coaching Mind-set

Great organizations understand the value of developing and investing in their employees. That said, these programs require an investment of time, energy, and resources, not to mention a financial commitment. It is the financial investment required that often stops organizations from using executive coaches. However, just as leadership development must be a strategic initiative, executive coaching must be a strategic part of leadership development.

Time and time again, I have observed that many organizations do not put enough emphasis, time, and investment into this area. While it is apparent the financial outlay required for executive coaching is significant, it must be included within the training and development budget, at the very least. Failure to bring in an outside coach and not have a group of coaches with different skill sets to work with the leadership team is extremely shortsighted. In order to fully develop its leaders, an organization must be committed to the learning process and the belief that people can benefit from the support and guidance of a skilled coach. Like everything else, the philosophy of creating a coaching culture and a coaching mind-set must come from the top and be reinforced from the top as well.

There must be a culture in place that embraces the concept of developing world class leaders and a model that holds the executives accountable. It is extremely important that the organization *does not* view coaching as an intervention to be used only when someone is in trouble or needs to improve some workplace skills. Coaching needs to be a proactive exercise, not reactive. Unfortunately, reactive coaching is the most common reason executive coaching takes place. When coaching is reactive, the coaching initiative is often too late in the process. When coaching is used as a last-ditch effort to help an individual, it is difficult to achieve positive outcomes because you are trying to coach someone who is on the bubble with a Performance Improvement Plan (PIP), or termination as the next step if changes are not made. Therefore, the person being coached is operating from fear, not success. When people are on the bubble and having trouble, it's often a sign that the individual is working in a job that isn't the right fit. While this is not 100 percent true, it is still a major reason that PIPs exist and coaching is used as the solution. Coaching needs to be used earlier on the front end to help the executive get off to a great start; coaches should not be brought in to do damage control but, unfortunately, it's the nature of the beast.

A simple analogy is driver's education. We don't just put the students behind the wheel and hope they don't hit anything. We put them in the classroom first, gradually expose them to driving on the open road, and then they take a driving test. We are often guilty of promoting someone without really evaluating his ability, or preparing and educating the person with the skills and competencies he needs to be successful. It's only after the individual fails that we take an active approach to help him, but by then the effort may be wasted.

The Case for an Executive Coach

"Give a man a fish, and he'll eat for a day.
Teach a man to fish, and he'll eat for a lifetime."

This long-standing aphorism says it all! Executive coaching is like teaching someone how to fish and obviously is a critical component of any leadership development program. There are many advantages to engaging an effective executive coach. Coaches can help employees because they can:

* see what others may not see

* step back to have enough distance to gain some perspective

* distinguish between a person's intentions and actions

* help the executive get past the self-deception caused by defensive thinking

* facilitate ways to develop new skill sets in a positive setting for growth

Great coaches present executives with an opportunity to engage in a dialogue of self-reflection and self-development. Leaders need a safe and supportive theater in which to rehearse and refine their ideas and perhaps even work through their issues. Leaders need someone to challenge them and someone who has the conviction to address the issues. Most importantly, the individual being coached needs someone who has no personal agenda or bias. This can only be accomplished through the use of an external coach.

Truly skilled coaches have the unique ability to get the most out of people. There are many great coaches from the sports world. If you follow basketball, you will remember the great John Wooden of UCLA, who won an unprecedented ten national championships. Then there are other great college coaches like Rick Pitino, now at the University of Louisville, and Mike Krzyzewski at Duke University. The NBA has greats like Red Auerbach, Phil Jackson, and Greg Popovich, just to name a few. The really great coaches stand out from the rest of the pack and have the unique ability to:

- create a readiness in others to change, learn, and grow
- facilitate a process to achieve a successful outcome
- move individuals into behaviors that sustain both short and long-term results

Executive coaching can help address barriers to an individual's growth and deliver sustained change. By using an objective third party, meaning an external coach, there is usually greater recognition of the issues by the individual who is being coached that sets the stage for increased receptivity for resolution and development. This is not to say there isn't a place for teaching managers how to develop their own coaching skills to strengthen their skills as a manager. There is a need for internal coaches, and some companies have developed internal coaching and mentoring programs to address that need. I think this is essential and something I highly support. I feel so strongly about this that I have created my own coursework on helping managers learn how to coach. However, developing an internal coaching program instead of going outside for a third-party objective coach is not an overall solution. The following explains why that entire philosophy is flawed.

An external coach can overcome barriers to professional development that internal coaches simply cannot. The greatest advantage to using an external coach is that it provides the executives someone in whom they can confide. Executives are more likely to reveal personal issues and be willing to admit they need to work on problems to an external coach than they would with an internal coach. An internal coach is more likely to make the executive feel vulnerable and exposed and, therefore, the executive may be less transparent and open to the coaching process.

The defining difference between an internal coach and an external coach is that the external coach can distance herself from the issues and the situation as well as the organization. Internal coaches are typically not equipped to handle this aspect of coaching. In addition, most organizations who provide training on coaching to their managers will find that while it can support the minor areas of coaching around the job content, most managers are not equipped to handle the coaching assignments when there are behavioral changes that need to be addressed, or when employees need to be prepared for promotions. These assignments need a coach who specializes in behavior or one who has the experience working with getting people ready for the next level or both, if the situation calls for it.

There Are Three Main Reasons for Coaching

1. Coaching for performance (overcoming challenges and encouraging growth)

2. Coaching for development (enhancing needed skills within the current role)

3. Coaching for advancement (developing new skill sets for the next role)

When you're considering providing coaching to someone it is worth exploring two concepts. First, as I discussed in the chapter on assessments, if more due diligence were spent on the front end evaluating an individual's potential via an evaluation and assessment process before hiring or promoting the person, the need for performance coaching would be reduced because you would have already validated the individual's ability. Often we hire or promote someone believing that he has the skills, competencies, and traits but not validating whether he actually does. More

165

importantly, we promote the person without giving him the proper tools and resources to be successful.

Second, if more time were spent coaching for development and advancement, perhaps there would be less need for coaching around performance. These views seem very obvious solutions to the development of staff but very little thought or credence is given to their utility. Again, this is why coaching needs to be proactive, not reactive. If more coaching were focused on development or preparing for advancement, there just might be a higher success rate when staff is promoted.

From my professional experience, the vast majority of coaching assignments I receive are because the executive is in crisis and struggling, or an intervention is needed, requiring a Performance Improvement Plan to be initiated. When coaching is introduced at this stage and the executive is asked to do a 360, complete some assessments, or any other action, the positive mental state that the executive needs to have is probably not the mind-set he currently possesses.

Sometimes the outcome of coaching is positive and sometimes it's not. If the person is in over his head, coaching may not be the answer. The possibility exists that the extent of the issue or issues is more dynamic and the individual would be better off with a therapist instead of a coach. I have seen this firsthand. In these instances, it is important to understand the level and sophistication of the assessment or assessments coaches use. This will tell you if they truly are capable of understanding someone's behavior at a deep enough level to grasp the extent of the problems and know what to do. Not many coaches can do this and it is important to understand why.

Most coaches believe they can coach anyone but, in reality, even having a very competent coach on the assignment won't change the outcome if there are deep behavioral challenges that need to be addressed. Take sports for an example. Why do great players get traded? Sometimes the trade is related to the salary cap, sometimes it's related to performance, but many times it's related to the players' behaviors. Recently, we have seen several teams in the NFL let players go because their behavior on and off the field interferes with their performance.

Perhaps you have heard or used the analogy, "You can't win the Kentucky Derby with a quarter horse." Some executives are simply in the wrong role and, in those situations, coaching is just not going to solve the problem. You don't have to know horses or horse racing to understand this simple concept. Likewise, putting the right people in the right roles, especially managerial roles, is important. Yet we continue to put people in the wrong roles and then rely on coaching to solve the problem. Coaching may be the answer on occasion but there are times when it isn't. Using the appropriate assessments, as I mentioned in chapter 6, lets you assess whether an individual is right for a particular role and whether a problematic situation can be corrected or not. This is the only way to really know if coaching will have an impact.

I emphasize this point because some coaches do not use assessments. And, even when they do, some coaches only use the four-dimensional assessments, such as the Myers-Briggs or the DiSC. However, these and all the other four-dimensional assessments are simply not robust enough for a higher-level coaching assignment, especially when behavioral issues are involved. Some coaches may be inclined to use a 360-degree assessment as their process. The problem with this approach is that the 360 generally will not tell you if an executive has any significant personality issues that would prevent him from succeeding, nor will the Myers-Briggs or any of the four-dimensional assessments currently on the market. Comments from the 360 may allude to some issues but a 360 is designed to get outside feedback and identify gaps in a person's competencies, not to determine any in-depth behavioral matters. Therefore, when choosing an executive coach you need to determine if the coach has the credentials and a viable process that can uncover the real issues and help bring about change. Just because a coach has a certification does not necessarily make him qualified for your particular situation.

In one high-level intervention in which I was involved, the executive was in so far over his head that no amount of coaching was going to rectify the situation. In another consultation, I was asked to coach an individual who had performance issues and I was supposed to ultimately prepare this person for advancement. My recommendation was not to promote the person because of the challenges she was facing at the time. My observations were supported by the peer interviews as well as my coaching time with the individual. In addition, the appropriate battery of assessments indicated the employee faced significant challenges that supported a decision to hold off a promotion. Even so, all this was ignored and the individual was promoted anyway. To the organization's credit, it hoped the individual would rise to the level of responsibility of the new position and that the promotion would resolve some of the issues. The executives thought that if they finally gave this individual the opportunity she sought, she would settle into the role. However, within six months of the promotion, the organization moved to terminate the employee for the very reasons I indicated. The behaviors played out as I suggested they would and the assessments used to uncover the behaviors I had concerns with were indicative of the behaviors that emerged.

In chapter 12, "Case Studies," I reference this coaching engagement as well as several others. There are many things a properly conducted assessment process can reveal and even help circumvent. Using the more sophisticated assessments like the 16PF Questionnaire or Hogan are far better coaching tools than any of the four-dimensional models. The true value of a properly designed assessment process can help solve problems regarding organizational development and job fit ahead of time and determine sooner rather than later if there are potential problems.

Mental Models–A Coach's Biggest Challenge

When I begin a coaching assignment, I want to know as much about the person I'm coaching as soon as possible.

I have experienced the difference between coaching assignments when people are totally engaged and others who just pay lip service until the coaching assignment has run its course. I want to get an understanding of what makes the person tick and what are the underlying issues. I need to understand their personality and their thinking style as well as their education, experience, and background. Assessments are an integral part of this process, and the right ones provide me with an immediate understanding of the depth of their personality. Assessments enable me to understand their mind-set from the start.

"By discovering our potential as human beings, we participate in the evolution of the human race. We develop the inner knowledge and wisdom required to guide our expectations. By studying our potential as human beings we may learn the ways to master the universe and ourselves."
—John Naisbitt, Author of *Megatrends*

Executive coaching offers a golden opportunity to help a person step back and reflect on his own personal and professional development. An executive coach can also help facilitate the person's self-awareness more effectively because of the third-party approach and the privacy created through the external coaching process. On the other hand, all coaches face a potential obstacle when working with clients. This obstacle is commonly referred to as a person's mental model.

We have a deep tendency to see the
changes we need to make as being in our
outer world, not in our inner world.

What this statement speaks to is a person's mind-set. That mind-set, what I refer to as the "mental model" of an executive, sometimes may be too much to overcome for the individual and often even for the coach. Here is an example of the power and impact of this concept. In one leadership development and coaching assignment, I facilitated the development of the president and his top seven senior executives of an Asian-owned, tier-one supplier in the automotive sector with the US division producing $600 million in revenue. They all went through the leadership development program including the assessments, peer reviews, and the 360 process. As part of the assignment, I was flown to the corporate office in Asia to conduct peer reviews and meet with the president, who was also the owner of the company. My meetings were peer reviews to discuss not only the development of the senior leadership staff in the United States, but the main goal was the development of the president of the US division and the accompanying challenges that needed to be addressed.

From the meetings and findings, I helped create a six-point development plan for the president of the US division. However, this president was reassigned six months later to a lesser role because he failed to act on any of the critical points presented in the findings and the initiatives outlined in the action plan. This person also failed to acknowledge the results of the entire process and was dumbfounded by the subsequent reassignment. In Asian cultures, the term "saving face" is common, so reassignments rather than demotions and termination are more common. The individual resigned shortly thereafter. Here are some more examples of what I mean by mental models.

Man blames fate for problems and accidents,
but feels personally responsible when
he makes a hole-in-one.

And my all-time favorite,

A person visits a therapist and says,
"I have just been fired for the fifth time in
seven years and I have been divorced
three times in the last five.

I desperately need you to help me understand
why are there so many screwed-up people out there?"

The obvious point I am trying to make with these examples regarding an executive's mental model is that everyone has preconceived notions that are based on their world and their own paradigms. Sometimes these paradigms need an adjustment and sometimes they need a major overhaul. The right coach will know what is needed and can make a tremendous difference.

Executive Coaching–A Process, Not an Event!

When I'm invited to coach someone, the question I'm asked most often is how long the process will take. There is no simple answer to this question. There are so many factors involved that it's hard to make any sort of prediction. The coaching process can be compared to a weight-loss program. Are you looking for some minor adjustments, such as losing a few pounds, or a major overhaul when you need to lose fifty and even 100 pounds, if not more? Take my example of the president of the Asian company who was demoted. This person made no attempt to work on the issues that came out of his 360 results and interviews. Whatever this executive's reasons, he refused to accept the results and was *unwilling* to work on the issues that were discussed during the entire leadership development process. Undoubtedly, denial and ego were major contributors to his eventual departure.

The next question I am asked: "How much does it cost?" Again, it's tricky to answer these queries since the determining factors come down to the severity of the situation and amount of time available. The most important factor is the desire and commitment from the executive to the process. The stronger the commitment and desire to improve the easier and faster the results. As I have mentioned, an effective coaching program requires an investment of both time and money. There are several different approaches coaches can use and the approach will obviously have an impact on the total investment. If you are going to take a Band-Aid approach, and use coaching to solve a performance or development problem, don't bother unless you're going to do it the right way because it will fail. You need a well-designed process that gives the coaching engagement a chance for success. My advice is not to use coaching as a means to an end. It is not good business sense and you will be wasting your investment.

Buy-In, Commitment, and Desire

How committed the executive is to the coaching experience varies from person to person. Great coaches need willing participants. There is an old adage which resembles coaching: "You can lead a horse to water but you can't make him drink, but you can salt the oats." The following statement really captures the essence of how important buy-in is to the process.

"A man won over against his will is
of the same opinion still."

Is the person approaching the coaching situation with his eyes wide open and a desire to learn or is he going through the motions because it is mandated by the organization? The right coach, with a well-designed coaching process, helps the individual become sensitized to act in a more purposeful way. Breakthrough thinking seldom occurs without people engaging in questions over a significant amount of time, as well as taking rigorous, experimental action in developing new skill sets and pursuing their goals.

Three Different Kinds of Coaches

In the field of medicine, doctors have specialties but they are all doctors of medicine. The same doctor you see to get a physical is not the same doctor you use to get a colonoscopy. That same doctor you saw for a colonoscopy will not be the same doctor you use when you have a heart problem. This is true of coaching as well. One size does not fit all, and there are various kinds of coaches with varying degrees of knowledge and expertise. We can identify three different kinds of coaches. I believe that each of them has its value and place in the coaching process:

- The life coach
- The business coach
- The behavior coach

Let me try to interject a little humor here. You may have heard the phrase, "Don't bring a knife to a gun fight." Well, as cliché as this old statement is, it has a high degree of relevance to selecting the right coach. Earlier I explained there are three different reasons for using a coach, and each situation requires the coach have a particular skill set. To help explain my point, one of my associates is an executive coach and he specializes in areas where the executive has substance abuse problems. Obviously, these problems can be very stressful and require someone who has experience and training in dealing with people with abuse issues.

While I am an experienced coach, this is not my expertise, and I would not accept a coaching assignment for someone whose problem is substance abuse.

■ The Life Coach

Some people need a life coach to help them figure out their career path and create new avenues for themselves. If an individual truly desires to change course, he will pursue a new avenue on his own or can engage a life coach. A life coach is not the kind of coach to be used in an intervention. It is important to evaluate the background for each coach you use to see what he or she has done that supports the coach's ability to make a difference for that executive based on the coaching assignment. If the individual has just gotten official certification as a life coach, he probably doesn't have the set of skills you need for your executive. The most significant reason for making the right coaching match is simple. If the person who is being coached does not believe the coach you have selected can make a difference and, more importantly, she does not respect the skills of the coach, the coaching assignment is doomed from the start.

■ The Business Coach

A business coach can address the issues of the executive who needs help and expertise with a certain skill set, discipline, and set of competencies. As an example, one of my coaching assignments was to help an executive prepare for a very senior role, the opportunity to become the next president of the company. He was the only internal candidate who was being considered for the position of president. The jury was still out as to whether he was the right candidate or whether the board should conduct an outside search. The current president decided he had two or three years before he retired. He also decided that over the course of the next year he would put this executive to the test.

Two problems existed. The executive had been with the organization a long time and he had been in a very senior role for a very long time as well. He was very well liked, respected, and extremely knowledgeable. He had done a respectable job of managing his department but, despite all his experience, he had failed to take a department that was optimizing its resources and its people to its fullest. There were several areas in which his department underperformed, which suggested that perhaps he was not presidential material, even though he was being considered for that position. If he couldn't lead the department to the next level, how would be lead the organization as president?

The next worry was that he was not "battle-tested." The concern was that he had never been president of any company; if he couldn't lead his current team to the next level, could he lead the organization to the next level? As his coach, we worked together to create two tracts for him to work on. One was focusing on how to shift from being a manager to a leader of his department and the other was putting him on an executive development path to prepare him for leading the organization. The goal was for him to develop the competencies necessary to lead the organization if he were chosen as the next president. This kind of coaching assignment would be well served by a coach who has either run his own business or had been a president of a company or both.

■ The Behavior Coach

An executive's behavior is often as challenging as the lack of business experience he or she has. When there are real behavioral issues, this coaching assignment is not for the typical business coach and especially not for a life coach. This kind of coaching requires someone who has extensive experience in analyzing human behavior at a deep enough level to help the executive understand what is happening and how to work through the issues.

Here is an example I used in chapter 6 about why assessments play an essential role in this area. If the person's assessment results show that this individual needs to be the center of attention, is overly dominant, and has a low tolerance for stress, you begin to create the feedback loop to help him see what he can't. The proper assessment, but more importantly a battery of quality assessments, can help assess the difference between someone who is full of himself because he is smarter than other people and needs to see how innocent celebrations might make others see him as egotistical versus someone who *is* egotistical and needs to be reminded of his imperfections. What you will come to realize is not many assessments can make the distinction between the two. And just as only a few assessments can make this distinction, neither can many executive coaches. This is especially true if they don't have an extensive background working on behavioral issues and either do not use an assessment when coaching or use one that isn't detailed enough to provide any significant insight.

I was once brought in to conduct an intervention in a coaching situation. The reasons for the executive's problem were based in behavior, not business. A business coach would not have the experience to provide value to the coaching process because he or she wouldn't have the experience or knowledge needed to engage the executive in the problem area. There are many scenarios around human behavior such as anger and aggression, dominate/dependent personality, and social dependency needs. Having the right assessment that can determine the depth of a person's anger or other behavior issues, and having the right behavioral coach to help the executive work through the dynamics is essential. In this example, a behavioral coach, not a life or business coach, is needed. The behavior coach needs to be able to evaluate what is happening to get at the heart of the issue. Getting at the depth of a person's issues is where the proper assessment process plays a role in coaching and a qualified behavioral coach is essential.

The Complexity Factor in Coaching

What happens when the executive needs coaching from both a business perspective and a behavioral perspective?

All too often this is the case. You either need a coach who can do both or you need two different coaches. It's important to evaluate the level of experience of the coach you're selecting to see if he or she will be able to make a difference. If you are engaging someone when behavior modification or a behavioral intervention is needed, then you need to find the appropriate coach with the right credentials. That particular coach needs to be able to decipher and understand whether the employee needs therapy. To explore this situation further, here are several questions you should ask any coach you're considering:

- Do you use any assessments to aid in the evaluation process, and which ones?

- What is your evaluation process?

- How many executives have you coached and over how long a period of time?

- What is your education, experience, and background, and how does it relate to the executive's needs?

By understanding the different aspects of coaching and the different kinds of coaches and their disciplines, you will be able to choose the coach you need for your specific situation. By choosing the right coach, you're more likely to have a better outcome for the employee and the company.

The Process—An Executive Coaching Outline

People will welcome the chance to learn to change their attitude or learn new skills and behavior when you make accurate assessments and supply observations to validate them. A proper coaching model helps initiate the transition that must take place and move the learning process along more rapidly. The goal should be to encourage breakthrough thinking by having people set stretch goals and asking them, "What's really possible to achieve?" Then it's important to craft a plan that shows them how to get there. I have created such a process and plan, and it is part of what I refer to as Strategic Leadership Assessment that was outlined in chapter 8. I use it in all my coaching assignments.

In Closing

While distinguishing the kind of coach you need with the experience to make a difference, you can't forget that if the executive being coached does not believe his assigned coach can help make a difference the coaching engagement is doomed for failure as well. When seeking out a coach make sure the coach has the credentials to support the coaching project. This kind of coaching assignment requires someone with the background extensive enough to accomplish your goals and objectives.

In order for coaching to be effective at an organizational level, it needs to be proactive not reactive. Establishing a coaching culture and a coaching mind-set is just the beginning. Teaching managers how to coach is essential and is another effective way to begin to change the culture, landscape, and mentality of your management team. It will help them move to be stronger coaches and mentors and develop new competencies. Beyond this internal coaching, there is also need for an external coach who is objective and can distance himself from the issues and the organization. You need to engage a coach with the background, experience, and expertise in the issues that need to be addressed. Providing an executive with a coach is an essential component in your world class leadership development program.

10

Linking the Pipeline with Succession Planning

Your pipeline feeds your succession planning process. Without a pipeline, you have no one to backfill vacancies and no one to fill newly created roles. Without a robust pipeline, succession planning becomes difficult, if not impossible. Major League Baseball has its farm teams that play in the minor leagues. The intent is to groom and prepare younger players to play in the majors and even rehabilitate longtime players. Your pipeline is the equivalent of your personal farm team, and you should use it to identify and groom talent. Your farm team is essentially your high-potential team. Your pipeline is the basis for succession planning and the two go hand in hand.

Building and Filling the Pipeline

If you recall my example in the beginning of the book, I mentioned that at the 1,000 largest American companies (by revenue) in 2008, eighty new CEOs were appointed, and only forty-four of them (55 percent) were promoted from within. While this data is dated not much has changed. All you need to do to track this trend is follow the Challenger, Gray & Christmas, Inc., *CEO Turnover Report*. But, to my point, if you view a board as having to go outside to hire a CEO as a failure in developing a strong pipeline that will support the succession planning process, it represents a breakdown in the system. A failure rate of 45 percent means that far too many succession plans aren't working. You need a pipeline of people to fill upcoming positions that may be created in the future or vacated by an aging population or by those who leave voluntarily or involuntary.

Hiring and the Selection Model—How It Supports the Pipeline

The best and easiest way to build your leadership pipeline is to hire the right people in the first place, not just the best available. The difference between hiring the right people and the best available rarely happens because we typically hire in haste to fill a vacated position. While having a selection model that enables you to hire the right people is simply a smart business strategy, this concept is often lacking. Most companies do not have a very sophisticated selection process, even though it ultimately contributes to filling the pipeline.

No business can fill its pipeline and, more importantly, no business can fulfill its potential, unless it gets the people process right. The right players take you to the

World Series or the Super Bowl; the wrong players get you looking for your next head coaching job. To that end, you simply have to hire right. The most popular statement that supports this premise is, "Put the right people on the bus and in the right seats," from the book, *Good to Great*. While this statement speaks for itself, it is extremely difficult to execute. You need to have a well-defined selection model to do so. You should ask yourself: what is the structure of your current selection process and is it good enough that you can hire great people? If not, what do you need to do to develop a world class selection model?

This chapter is not about how to develop a strong selection model, but I need to take a moment to speak about this concern. Without a forward-thinking selection model, filling the pipeline becomes more challenging. When you build out your staffing plans, you should evaluate the talent pool you will need going forward. You must have an eye toward hiring for today as well as filling the pipeline for tomorrow. It is important to ask key questions as you begin to recruit and bring in new talent:

- Do we have a well-defined staffing plan? How do we know? What should it look like? Are we using the right tools to evaluate the talent we are bringing in?

- Do we have the right process in place to assure we are hiring right?

- Who is retiring soon and can they be easily replaced?

- Who has been underperforming? Do they need to be moved to a role that is more complementary to their skills or do they need to be replaced?

- What new openings are going to emerge as the company expands? Which skill sets will be needed?

- What skills, behaviors, and core values do we, as a company, want to use for our selection parameters?

- Can the competency profile we seek be trained or must certain characteristics be intrinsic?

- What will the job be like tomorrow and will the person be able to handle it? If not, what does he need to do differently?

- Do we have a staffing model and selection system that will help assure we have the right talent?

- Do our managers know how to interview effectively? Have they been properly trained on how to interview?

- Do we know if we are using the proper assessments that get us closer to the right candidates or using ones that are convenient just to have something in place?

We're often so focused on filling a position in the immediate future because there is work that needs to be completed, but we wind up hiring in haste. We are so intent on what we need right now that we don't evaluate what we will need in the role for the future. Because we don't have a solid selection system in place, we wind up hiring someone only to find out later that he or she doesn't have what it takes for the current role, let alone the future role. A great hiring process, if well defined, will tell you if you are hiring for the future. That subject requires another book, but one way to evaluate whether or not you are on track is to go back and review chapter 6, "Exploring the World of Assessments." Using the appropriate assessments is one of the most critical components of a great selection process.

Talent Management
Who Is Capable of Filling the Pipeline?

The other way to fill the leadership pipeline is quite obvious. Examine potential internal candidates among your current personnel. Without a plan in place that evaluates the available talent pool effectively, you'll end up sending the wrong message when unqualified people wind up on the high-potential list. In organizations today it is not uncommon to find a program called the High Potential Group (HIPOs). People get nominated or appointed into this elite group for various reasons. Some people get into this elite group the right way, through performance. Others get in the wrong way. When people get in the wrong way the integrity of the high-potential program gets devalued. Let's take longevity. When people who have been at the organization for a very long time and supposedly deserve the next promotion are nominated into this group or promoted, that's the wrong way.

Sometimes someone is very nice and seems capable and gets into this group. In other cases, someone knows someone in power and gets in because of politics. Getting into this group by being a friend of a friend is bad enough, but the worst one of them all is nepotism. I have seen the aftermath of this when entitlement, rather than performance, comes into play. When people get nominated into this elite group by anything other than performance it just diminishes the program and misses the whole point. Establishing your pipeline and building a high-potential program should be for the elite whose performance has been stellar.

All kinds of people get placed into the high-potential pool, some are qualified and many are not particularly qualified. Once when I was working with a company, there were nearly eighty high-potential managers, and many people wondered how some of these people got into this pool. We performed the assessments and helped conduct the evaluations and development plans for all of the executives. I, myself, questioned how some of them were on the list after conducting the evaluations. We even created an entire training and development matrix for their development. I was fortunate enough to execute this program from the start when the organization had no formalized way to identify its talent. There was a tremendous amount of animosity when certain people emerged on the high-potential list, those whom colleagues felt did not belong, while their colleagues were passed over. You are going to have a certain amount of gossip and office politics as that is simply human nature. But, if you lay out the program correctly, you lessen the possibility of resentment among the employees. Here is how we begin to lay out a strategy for identifying high-potential prospects to evaluate where future leaders will come from.

To begin the process we need to evaluate who you have, what they have done, and where they have shown promise. The questions that help gauge this are:

- Are my leaders functioning as well as they can?

- Are my results where they should be?

- Who are my leaders today? Are they ready now?

- Who are my leaders for tomorrow? What will it take to prepare them?

- Where are my weakest links? Can they be strengthened?

- How committed is each member of the team?

- Can they identify, articulate, and implement the goals and objectives?

- Where have they demonstrated promise and above average results in their role?

- How do we really know they are capable of functioning at the next level?

As you begin to ask and answer these questions about your current staff, you will begin to realize two things. One is what the staffing plan needs to look like going forward and the other is what the developmental plan needs to be in order to get the people you have performing at a higher level.

Critical Talent–The Basis for Building a Pipeline

"Critical Talent" refers to those individuals who are the drivers of your company's business performance and generate greater than average value for customers and shareholders. Managing your talent is one sure way to stay progressive and competitive. Identifying and finding critical talent is a significant issue, but it isn't enough. Assessing, developing, and training are essential elements in the scope of talent management as well. Perhaps your biggest challenge of all is retaining that talent. Assessing and developing your internal and external talent and their needs can help open the path for growth. It will increase your bench strength and help you retain your best and brightest for the long term.

In my leadership work, I conduct a program called "Three-Dimensional Leadership–Developing the Leader Within," which I discussed in chapter 7. During the program I always ask the attendees, "Do you have your replacement in place and, if so, are you grooming him or her to take over when you move up in responsibility?" I am amazed that the vast majority of the time the answer is, "No, I don't."

This is a simple problem that must be corrected or your pipeline will remain bleak. You should be looking at all supervisory and management positions in the company and evaluating the abilities of those individuals in the roles. In addition, you need to be evaluating who is next in line so you are grooming those people along the way as well. The goal is to not have to hire from the outside to fill the void. Most of the time this isn't the case. Managing the talent pool needs to be a strategic initiative to continue to stay competitive. The cost of turnover is too great, at two-and-a-half times a person's annual salary, so mistakes need to be minimized. With constant turnover, you never gain the depth of knowledge about the company or the products to be effective; all that knowledge is lost when that tenured person leaves.

It is important to establish the parameters and structure that need to be created through which successful leaders will be developed. This will provide a sustained, balanced system that will fulfill the organizational needs. It's no secret that leaders are made, not born. This is all the more reason to understand what it takes to create a high-potential program that fills the pipeline. It is imperative to conduct regular workforce planning discussions with functional managers. It is important to explore the best way to create a high-potential program. To do so we need to:

- develop and present a long-term forecast of human capital needs at the organizational level;

- develop the parameters around creating a high-potential pool of individuals, and stay away from popularity contests as a means to fill the pipeline;

- identify those who can and cannot succeed in their current assignments and what to do about it;

- focus on the key transition points in the evolution of managers to leaders and the link to an organization's strategic intent and the competencies required for success; and

- evaluate why managers are underperforming at their current level and how to help them and the organization manage the situation.

At a more strategic level, we must answer these questions:

- Which strategies, skills, and capabilities are crucial to our current and future success?

- How can we identify those who can and cannot succeed when they advance into larger assignments, such as an international assignment?

- What emerging workforce trends (e.g., supply and demand of engineers) will impact our ability to deliver value?

- Who supports our critical segments of talent within their network? Are these supporting people difficult to replace?

- Within our workforce who possesses the greatest current and future potential?

Development and Its Impact on Filling the Pipeline

Once we have identified the high-potential people and filled the pipeline, we need to identify the skills, competencies, and behaviors we want them to develop so they will be prepared for the next level or levels. This is where the Three-Dimensional Leadership model comes into play. Making sure to develop the whole person is essential to the person's future success. It's knowing that once a person is placed in a given role, he or she will have an opportunity to develop further. Now is the time to move the professional development process into another level by establishing the developmental plans to close the gaps.

Succession Planning

Out of nowhere the president resigns and takes another role or the existing president is forced to resign. The vice president of engineering up and decides to take an early retirement. The CFO suddenly passes away. An executive makes a political blunder. These things happen all the time. When they happen at your organization, will you have to go outside the organization or do you have a succession plan in place? Succession planning is different from creating a pipeline. Building a pipeline consists of identifying and recruiting the right talent, whereas succession planning is identifying the developmental needs of the talent within the high-potential pool. Succession planning looks at the talent and evaluates the developmental needs required for the various roles people will be elevated to as they advance through the organization. In most companies, these two practices reside in separate functional silos, if at all, but they are natural allies. This is because they share a vital and fundamental goal: getting the right people with the right skills in the right place.

To become a Navy SEAL, the strongest and the fittest of current Navy personnel are selected and put into a rigorous training regimen to see who will make it through some of the toughest training in the world. This training is aimed at determining who are the most capable of becoming a Navy SEAL. Most wash out before completing the program.

Succession planning is a process for identifying the developmental needs of internal people with the potential to fill key business leadership positions in the company. Succession planning increases the availability of experienced and capable employees who are prepared to assume these roles as they become available. There is a big difference between a basic replacement plan and a robust succession plan for cultivating individuals for key leadership roles. A leadership competency model is required to structure the talent management processes throughout the employee lifecycle that supports succession planning. Succession planning and the leadership development's initiative is to create a long-term process for managing and developing the talent across the organization. A successful outcome requires the strategic application of integrated technical tools and systems for performance management that supports succession planning and leadership development.

Some basic requirements of the organization to help support the pipeline and the succession planning process would be:

- Engage the leadership in supporting the development of high-potential leaders.

- Build a database of up-and-comers that can be used to make better staffing decisions for key jobs.

- Identify those with the potential to assume greater responsibility.

- Provide critical development experiences to those who are able to move up.

- Improve employee commitment and retention.

- Meet the career development expectations of existing employees.

- Counter the increasing difficulty and costs of recruiting employees externally.

In Closing

An organization's pipeline feeds their succession planning process. No business can fill its pipeline until it gets the people process right. To do so requires a robust, well-defined selection model with an eye toward hiring for today and filling the pipeline for tomorrow. Succession management must be a flexible system oriented toward developmental activities, not a rigid list of high-potential employees and the slots they might fill. By marrying succession planning and leadership development, you get the best of both worlds. Paying attention to the skills required for senior management positions, along with an educational system that can help managers develop those skills, is essential.

11

The Unknown Element
Human Behavior and Its Impact on Leadership

What is the measure of a leader? What are the behaviors that differentiate the successful leader from the less successful leader? Why are some leaders more successful than others? This chapter will examine the behaviors that distinguish successful leaders from not-so-successful leaders.

In the beginning of this book I presented examples of fallen leaders and provided some insight into challenges they faced that ultimately contributed to their downfall. There were obvious reasons these people were promoted into those senior leadership roles; but the more obvious set of dynamics is that they could not overcome the challenges they faced. Some were publicized while others were not, making it difficult for an outsider to understand what went wrong, but the fact that these were high-profile people, in high-profile companies, who were asked to resign by the very board who selected them, indicates something indeed was wrong. The outcome tells us their leadership was somehow flawed. Their results also show us the decision to promote them was flawed. Somewhere between their behavioral tendencies and a lack of competencies, there were certain dynamics that they could not overcome.

Particularly telling is that Ivester of Coca-Cola and Barad of Mattel were targeted as successors to their predecessors. They were highly valued, highly recognized, and highly thought of internal individuals who were promoted to the next level but, shortly thereafter, they failed badly. It proves that the Peter Principle is real. It also validates my theory that if a leader does not recognize and work toward identifying his behavior, and understand how his behavior impacts his leadership style and also does not identify any potential gaps, let alone acknowledge them, there are likely to be challenges ahead. Leaders must identify where their gaps are and work on developing these areas. If not careful, their ego and title, among other things, may eventually do them in. For these reasons, a strong leadership assessment process and a comprehensive leadership development evaluation is necessary to help assess whether an individual has the skills and traits needed to excel at a higher level.

Too often we blindly promote someone we believe can manage at the next level, but we really don't have an accurate way of knowing whether that person can succeed, as was evident with the Coca-Cola and Mattel scenarios. This further supports the need to conduct a Strategic Leadership Assessment, even on people we *think* we know. I am sure that the boards of Coca-Cola and Mattel felt they knew these individuals well enough to promote them but, obviously, they missed something. I bet many of you have also promoted someone who didn't work out as well as you expected. The question to ask is, "What didn't I see coming and why?"

This chapter focuses on the behaviors that can derail an executive. The next chapter will present case studies of people from various leadership roles with whom I have had direct involvement. Here I will offer insight into their behaviors. These case studies will explain how different behaviors impacted both the successful executives and the less successful ones. The case studies will also help to show how the predictability of a well-constructed battery of assessments is preferable to any single assessment and why a robust assessment process is necessary to help identify and develop successful leaders.

Whether in hiring or promoting individuals, in my research, no single instrument is effective as an assessment tool. There are some that come close. For instance, the 16PF Questionnaire is one of the most comprehensive and sophisticated instruments on the market and is my preferred choice; however I still do not rely on it solely for every situation. You will need the information provided by the 16PF Questionnaire and supported by additional assessment results to thoroughly evaluate the future potential of your leaders. You will see how the battery of assessments provided information that was used to predict certain behaviors in the case studies I present in chapter 12.

Human Behavior

If behavior is the single biggest predictor of performance, then it stands to reason the more we know about someone's

behavior the greater chance we have of hiring and promoting the right person. When we hire someone there
are a number of unknowns. The most notable is what the
person's true behavior is, especially under pressure. What
we don't know is how he or she will perform once in the
role, whether there are any knowledge or experience gaps,
and what the person is capable of. You really cannot tell
any of these things until the person steps into the role.
When you really stop and think about it, almost everything
about the person is an unknown. This is where a battery
of assessments can bridge the gap.

Remember my example of the service manager who
became branch manager and nearly caused the staff to orga-
nize a union? It is safe to assume that the organization felt it
knew him well enough and saw him as a favorable candidate
for promotion. This example again shows that it's almost
impossible to say you know someone really well until that
person is put into a new role and you see how he performs.

In the examples of the service manager who became
branch manager, and the executives from Coca-Cola and
Mattel, the leaders were internal candidates who were
seen as ideal choices to be promoted. In some ways they
were a known entity but, as the results show, there were
still many unknowns. When you look at any new hire,
especially for a senior leadership position, everything is
suspect because you can't trust the résumé and you can't
assume everything the candidate told you in the interview
is true. You may be impressed with the credentials and
previous positions but the person's behavior remains a

big unknown. (Pay close attention to "Case Study 12.5" in chapter 12.) In most selection models there is little focus on understanding an individual's behavior as part of the model. Even those who use a behavior-based interview process will miss many undesirable behaviors. If you think about the difference between why we hire and why we fire, you can see the relevance behind this comparison. It is an inherent flaw in the process.

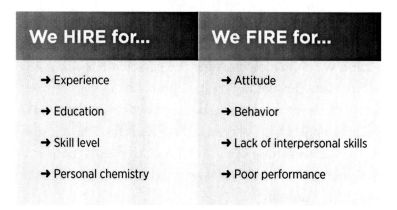

We HIRE for...	We FIRE for...
→ Experience	→ Attitude
→ Education	→ Behavior
→ Skill level	→ Lack of interpersonal skills
→ Personal chemistry	→ Poor performance

Table 11.1 Comparison Why We Hire / Why We Fire

We are guilty of all sorts of interview mistakes and hiring inefficiencies that lead us to missteps in the selection process. The difference between how we hire and how we fire may be responsible for all hiring mistakes.

The Three Biggest Hiring Myths

I wish I had a dollar for every time I have heard comments like, "I'm a pretty good judge of character," or "I can read people pretty well," and "I know a good one when I see one." These are three of the biggest fallacies and myths to ever come out of the hiring process. They're just foolish comments. Let me explain why. I have listed here some examples of the behaviors that often get in the way of an individual's performance. These behaviors will create problems in any position, not just a leadership role. After you read through the behaviors, ask yourself if you are astute enough to pick out these behaviors in an interview. If you're honest you will recognize that these behaviors are impossible to pick out during the interview process. I think we can safely assume the candidate is not going to talk about any of his faults. The odds are even greater that if there are any issues, they will not be exposed in the reference-checking process, either. Therefore, it's a guessing game, and there is no way you can predict someone else's behavior, no matter how good a judge of character you think you are.

During an interview you are witnessing an individual's behavior in a setting that is entirely different from the workplace. If you were attempting to hire someone from outside the organization to fill a leadership role, or any role for that matter, how would you know if there were any of these behavioral issues present? As you read through the behaviors listed on the following page, ask yourself, "Can I honestly pick out these behaviors in an interview?" To further challenge yourself, consider asking, "Can I determine how deep seeded the behavior really is?"

- High need for social approval

- High need to impress with low need for approval

- Does not pick up on social cues of others

- May not possess enough self-insight

- Over-engages conversations/Is a poor listener

- Makes decisions in isolation of others

- Can be harsh and unemotional

- Anger and aggressive tendencies

- High need for change and control

- Passive/Aggressive

- Dominate/Dependent

- Will alienate people

- Egotistical/Arrogant/Self-serving

- Condescending/Talks down to others

It is highly unlikely you can pick out these behaviors during an interview, let alone know whether they are deeply ingrained. It is a given the candidate is going to be on his or her best behavior in the interview. During that time you are not witnessing how the candidate behaves in a work environment. Furthermore, even if you hire the person, the behaviors rarely show up right away. These behaviors usually begin to surface three to six months after you hire someone. However, it's possible these behaviors will not show up for quite some time. The possibility exists that these tendencies will show up and be more evident or pronounced only when an individual progresses in responsibilities, roles, and title. As responsibilities and roles increase and stress is added, changes in someone's behavior may start to emerge.

The same rules apply to internal candidates as we prepare them for advanced roles because, as with the service manager who became branch manager, you never know how they will perform until they are actually in the role. To reinforce this go back and read the details around Ivester's and Barad's terminations.

If we spent more time understanding the behaviors of people before we hired them, and especially before we promoted them, we probably would have fewer problems related to performance management issues and having to place people on PIPs. Likewise, if we spent more time understanding the behaviors of people before we promoted them, we would have fewer missteps. The consequences of hiring and promoting individuals with behavioral and other problems are obviously quite costly for many reasons.

There are only a very few assessments on the market that can pick out these tendencies as I explained in chapter 6. However the 16PF Questionnaire is very effective at doing so. Refer to Table 11.2 to understand more about the sixteen factors and their meanings.

16PF FACTORS

FACTOR	LEFT MEANING (-)	RIGHT MEANING (+)
A	Reserved, Impersonal, Distant	Warm, Outgoing, Attentive to Others
B	Concrete	Abstract
C	Reactive, Emotionally Changeable	Emotionally Stable, Adaptive, Mature
E	Cooperative, Avoids Conflict	Dominant, Forceful, Assertive
F	Serious, Restrained, Careful	Lively, Animated, Assertive
G	Expedient, Nonconforming	Rule-Conscious, Dutiful
H	Shy, Threat-Sensitive, Timid	Socially Bold, Venturesome
I	Utilitarian, Objective, Unsentimental	Sensitive, Aesthetic, Sentimental
L	Trusting, Unsuspecting, Accepting	Vigilant, Suspicious, Skeptical, Wary
M	Grounded, Practical, Solution-Oriented	Abstracted, Imaginative, Idea-Oriented
N	Forthright, Genuine, Artless	Private, Discreet, Non-Disclosing
O	Self-Assured, Unworried, Complacent	Apprehensive, Self-Doubting, Worried
Q1	Traditional, Attached to Familiar	Open to Change, Experimenting
Q2	Group-Oriented, Affiliative	Self-Reliant, Solitary, Individualistic
Q3	Tolerates Disorder, Flexible	Perfectionist, Self-Disciplined
Q4	Relaxed, Placid, Patient	Tense, High Energy, Impatient, Driven

Table 11.2 Left and Right Meaning 16PF Behavior Factors[4]

These sixteen factors are very telling when it comes to understanding someone's personality and how the person will likely behave. The real value is in the combinations of the individual factors. When used in combination, they create an even more revealing set of dynamics about a person. This is what makes the 16PF Questionnaire so powerful. It's the combination of certain traits from the 16PF Questionnaire that will tell us if these behaviors are part of someone's personality and how deeply they might run. The behaviors I have listed can be captured and

---

[4] Adapted with permission from the Institute for Personality and Ability Testing, Inc. (2009). 16PF Fifth Edition Questionnaire Manual. Savoy, IL.

quantified by the characteristics that make up the 16PF Questionnaire. A well-designed assessment can give you this depth of insight. Utilizing the combinations of factor analysis, the behaviors that I listed can be identified pre-hire or prepromotion by evaluating someone's assessment results. The previous behaviors I gave you can be identified by utilizing the combinations of factor analysis using the 16PF traits. Here are the combination factors that go together to predict these behaviors:

- A+ Q2– High need for social approval

- H+ A– High need to impress with low need for approval

- H+ I– Does not pick up on social cues of others

- H+ O– May not possess enough self-insight

- H+ N– Overengages in conversations/is a poor listener

- A– Q2+ Makes decisions in isolation of others

- E+ I– Can be harsh and unemotional

- E+ L+ Anger and aggressive tendencies

- E+ Q1+ High need for change and control

- E– L+ Passive-aggressive

- E+ Q2– Dominate/Dependent

- L+ A– Will alienate people

- E+ H+ O– Egotistical

- E+ L+ A– Critical and condescending to others

As I have mentioned before, the vast majority of assessments simply cannot pick out these behaviors. Any four-dimensional instrument, such as the DiSC, Predictive Index, MBTI, Birkman, and others only measure four traits. Even the Profiles XT and the Caliper cannot reach deep enough because they don't measure workplace coping skills, which is the Anxiety domain from the 16PF Questionnaire. To further support the need for an assessment process that supports a world class leadership development program, and to make sure you are not promoting people to positions over their heads, here are some more examples of extreme behaviors that show the importance of using a more sophisticated assessment process. Every combination of the traits I have listed will have either a positive or a potentially negative impact on the effectiveness of someone's leadership ability. We are then searching for the right balance of behaviors in our leaders. As traits combine with one another, we can assess deeper behaviors that may be present.

The behaviors listed here are relevant to a person's leadership style and leadership results. Let's take the first example I listed.

- *A+ Q2– High need for social approval*

A+ (Warmth) scores of 8, 9, or 10 are indicative of people who express a warmth toward others, value friendship, as well as value dealing and working with people. They tend to build trust easily. Scores on Q2– (Team player) of 1, 2, or 3 are indicative of people who like working with groups and tend to see value in working together. What the combination of these two scores reveals about an individual is that in their interactions they tend to warm up to others quickly and are highly supportive of people. The downside is that they may be more interested in getting along with their peers and subordinates than holding them accountable or dealing with conflict because these traits indicate people who are conflict-avoidant. In addition, they may have a hard time disciplining others because the need to be liked is greater than the stress of potentially alienating someone or hurting their feelings. This is compounded if scores of I+ (Sensitive) and O+ (Worrisome) are present in the profile as well.

Here are a few more examples of the predictive nature of the 16PF Questionnaire using multiple factor analysis. The following combinations are more complex and can help you begin to understand the true range of the 16PF Questionnaire and its sophistication.

- F+, H+, G–, Q3– Needs to have fun and explore but hates society rules and bucks the system with no internal self-discipline to offset the need for fun.

- E+, L+, Q1+ Aggressive and angry at the world, has a chip on his shoulder, and prone to argue and even fight.

- C–, O+ Does not cope with things in general, places a lot of self-imposed stress on themselves.

- I+, M+, Q1+, C– Idealist who is out of touch with reality.

- E–, F–, O+, C– The world is bigger than them and they don't know how to cope with it.

- O+, F–, E–, C– Somber person who has little self-esteem and is down on life in general.

- O+, F–, L+, C– Sees the world as hostile and negative and not fun so life becomes more challenging.

- E+, L+, Q4+ Highly impatient and critical of others and things surrounding their worlds.

Let's take a deeper look at the last combination of scores as another point of reference:

- *E+, L+, Q4+ Highly impatient and critical of others and things surrounding their worlds.*

The combination of these three traits is fairly common in many leaders. People who have an E+ score of 8, 9, or 10 are assertive, competitive, driven with a desire to lead or be in control, and take pride in their ability to have a dominant presence over others. An L+ score of 8, 9, or 10 is indicative of people who don't trust things and are always challenging conventional wisdom and strive to make things better. A score of Q4+ with an 8, 9, or 10 suggests people who display a high degree of impatience. Often, these people are impatient with others who don't move as fast as they do and they also have high demands and expectations for instant results. If the scores of these three factors are all high, a person will display traits that are much more demonstrative than if all three scores are moderate. The concern is when the inherent traits are too much of a bad thing, which would set the stage for disaster. If the factors are within an acceptable range then, with some coaching and development, individuals can be effective versus ineffective. If all three factors are extremely high, you will likely have morale and turnover issues at the expense of results. In other words, with scores of E10, L10, and Q4/10, the combination of these three behaviors will represent a much stronger personality than someone with scores of E7, L7, and Q4/7.

This is only a small sampling of what can be revealed when you look at all of the combinations attainable from the sixteen factors, but the relevance has significant impact in a person's leadership ability, as you will see when you read the case studies. For a deeper understanding of the combination of factors I suggest you read Dr. Michael Karson's book, *16PF in Clinical Practice*; Dr. James Schuerger and Dr. Heather Cattell's book, *Essentials of 16PF Assessment*; and Wendy Lord's two books, *Personality in Practice* and *Overcoming Obstacles to Interpretation* that were referred to in chapter 6.

In addition to the case studies, it is important you understand how the battery of assessments I've been referring to can provide additional insight into an individual's capabilities and capacity. By grasping more of an individual's personality, behavioral makeup, thinking styles, emotional intelligence, and cognitive reasoning skills, you can begin to assess whether or not an individual has the necessary traits to be successful in rising through the various levels of leadership. Knowing how behavior impacts leadership is essential. Together, the process of evaluating behavior and critical thinking skills helps form the basis and the beginning stages of identifying high-potential candidates to fill your pipeline for future leadership positions.

Not only can you begin to make some assumptions about whether an individual has the ability to succeed, you can see whether he has the capability to develop himself and understand how far he can go. I discussed different scenarios around an individual's personality, such as the ability to cope with the challenges, dealing with ambiguity, or having the flexibility to manage change. These are just a few of the behaviors that can derail an individual in any role, but especially in a leadership role. Some of these traits are coachable but some require counseling that goes beyond the work done by the typical executive coach. This is why you should use an executive coach who has been trained in behavior and who uses the proper assessment tools. Remember, just because an executive coach is certified by one of the many coaching certification programs does not mean he or she has the skill sets to coach the kinds of behavior issues I have presented here.

When we study the qualities of successful leaders we find that eleven of the 16PF traits are the most relevant traits that are consistent with high-performing leaders. As you will see in the case studies, these factors are consistent with what will be discussed when comparing those who have been successful with those who haven't.

Eleven Core Traits of Successful Leaders[5]

- A+ Warmth

- B+ High Reasoning

- C+ Emotional Balance

- E+ Competitiveness/Drive

- F+ Spontaneity

- G+ Conscientious

- H+ Social Boldness

- O- Self-Confidence

- I+ Intuition

- M+ Creativity

- Q1+ Readiness for change

---

[5] "Leadership Study: Analysis of High Potential Managers" (2001–2002), Data analysis from the 16PF Questionnaire, conducted by The Executive Group, Rick Tiemann.

These eleven core traits are highly identified behaviors in successful leaders. As we evaluate each trait on its own merit, each has a significant effect on the results you would look to have from your leaders. Imagine a leader with little emotional balance having a score of C– versus C+. One of the case studies I include shows how this dynamic trait manifests itself in an individual's leadership presence and the problems it causes. There are many combinations but one truth emerges: behavior is a critical part of assessing a leader's potential.

You will see some of these traits play out in the case studies with the corresponding assessment results that I refer to as profiles. I will discuss the use of incorporating a battery of various assessments, how they play a part in understanding a person's makeup, and the impact this has on his leadership skills. The value of this information will not only aid in the selection process but also in the promotion, development, and succession planning process.

Through the use of an in-depth assessment like the 16PF Questionnaire, you can get a more thorough understanding of the individual's behavioral makeup. When you use additional assessments, you have comparative data to validate other information you see among the various instruments. By the same token, by using multiple assessments you are able to see any differences in behavior that stand out from one assessment to the other. Another significant benefit to using multiple assessments is that it becomes harder for the person to manipulate the results.

There are six assessments in our Executive Battery when we conduct a leadership assessment. Three assessments measure personality and behavior and three measuring critical thinking skills. Included in the three behavior and personality assessments we use are the 16PF Questionnaire, Hogan, and the DiSC. These are used in combination to support the integrity of the data about an individual's personality traits. This helps weed out any distortion and test-taking mentality that might exist. What is meant by *test-taking mentality* is whether the individual is trying to alter the outcome of the results. I am looking for consistencies as well as inconsistencies between the assessments results.

You can refer back to chapter 6 for more insight into this. In the case studies you will notice that the DiSC instrument is another tool I use in the battery of assessments. While I mentioned earlier that the DiSC is not designed as a standalone tool for selection or true leadership development, it still provides a supporting and confirming scan at relevant behaviors in an evaluation process when used with other tools. The information from the 16PF Questionnaire, Hogan, and the DiSC should correlate when someone takes all three. This means if you see assertive tendencies in the 16PF Questionnaire, you should see assertive tendencies in the Hogan and the DiSC as well.

Another example would be if you see a very social person on the 16PF Questionnaire, you should see a very social person on the Hogan and the DiSC as well. The difference being that the 16PF Questionnaire breaks down the assertive tendencies or social tendencies into more finite detail. When the 16PF Questionnaire and the DiSC do not correlate, there may be other dynamics present. There are some traits, such as tough-mindedness, emotional resilience, and reasoning that the DiSC does not measure but the 16PF Questionnaire does. While the Hogan doesn't have a reasoning component it does explore behaviors that can inhibit leadership effectiveness. Any inconsistencies need to be examined in order to confirm specific traits. When the traits you would expect to see on the 16PF Questionnaire, Hogan, and the DiSC don't match, you will have to do further evaluation. The traits should align. If they don't, it's likely that something is going on with the individual. This is why trying to use one assessment in evaluating and developing your leaders is not sufficient. It is especially important when you are evaluating an external candidate for a leadership position because you know even less about an outside hire. Utilizing a sophisticated battery of assessments reduces the risk of a bad hire or a mistaken promotion because the most costly hire, next to sales, is in management and senior leadership roles.

While the DiSC is less sophisticated than the 16PF Questionnaire or the Hogan, it has a unique benefit. The structure of the DiSC instrument utilizes three graphs as a representation to describe personality. When there is a difference in the patterns of the first and second graphs it suggests inconsistent behaviors are present. When you use multiple assessments it is harder for an individual to try to outsmart the assessments. The more assessments you use the easier it is to begin to interpret any concerning behavioral issues. By adding the Hogan to the mix, you are able to compare how the 16PF Questionnaire and the Hogan line up. I have found that the 16PF Questionnaire, Hogan and DiSC, when combined together, bring a powerful validation component that is unmatched by any individual instrument. The case studies will show the significance of interpreting the information from the three assessments.

Besides measuring behavior and the emotional components, we can gauge a number of ways in which a person processes information. To help measure someone's problem-solving and critical thinking skills, we use three additional assessments in our Executive Battery as well. The DiSC and the Hogan do not measure reasoning and problem-solving ability, but the 16PF Questionnaire does. Beyond the measure of problem solving within the 16PF Questionnaire, we use three additional problem-solving assessments. The first assessment is referred to as a "Cultural Fair" instrument, meaning it is culturally fair because it does not discriminate based on an individual's cultural background, education, or gender. This instrument measures a person's perceptual reasoning and helps in revealing his potential learning ability and rate of processing speed.

The second instrument we use measures a person's inductive and deductive reasoning. It has forty problems and measures five categories including how a person draws conclusions, interprets information, makes assumptions, builds a case for arguments, and draws an inference around a subject or an issue. People who score higher on this assessment are typically bright, strong problem solvers, and highly abstract thinkers. People who score low on this assessment are more inclined to struggle with more complex issues. Extremely low scorers may not always be the most adept at making sound decisions and need more time or someone with whom to consult.

The third assessment we use is a 126-item timed test of general mental ability that looks at mental agility and flexibility. It measures an individual's capacity to acquire new knowledge and skills and apply them to problem solving. It also measures individual differences in the ability to perform mental tasks of varying types and complexity. Four job-related tasks are assessed, including adjusting to new situations, learning new skills quickly, understanding complex or subtle relationships, and thinking flexibly. Questions are arranged in order of increasing difficulty in the following sequence: two verbal (linguistic) items, one quantitative (math) item; two verbal items, two quantitative items; and two verbal problems activating alternate left brain/right brain activity.

People in roles like accounting in theory should generally score higher on the quantitative section. By the same token, people who are journalists should generally score higher on the verbal scales. People who score low on both scales may be slow, methodical readers or have other issues such as being paralyzed by taking a timed test. Those who score high are usually well read and able to think very quickly on their feet. They are generally more articulate and faster at analyzing data. Those people who score low may not like to make mistakes and, consequently, are extremely thorough and methodical. This type of individual is less likely to do well on this assessment because of the timed element.

Understanding the correlation between the inductive and deductive reasoning test, the perceptual reasoning test, and the cognitive reasoning test can provide a portrait of an individual's true intellectual ability and how strong his ability is in decision making and problem solving. By combining the personality traits and the reasoning and problem-solving ability of an individual, you can begin to gain insight into how well he will perform in a leadership role and whether the Peter Principle might apply in the future.

In Closing

I cannot emphasize this enough that behavior is the biggest predictor of performance and has a tremendous impact on an individual's success in a corporate setting. Being able to assess the behaviors of the future leaders of your organization is a critical step in filling the leadership pipeline. By conducting a thorough assessment of an individual's traits, you will not only be successful in filling the pipeline with higher-caliber people, you will know who has the ability to perform at the next level and, therefore, can choose people for promotions who are ready for future challenges.

12

Case Studies

How Behavior and Critical Thinking Skills
Impact Leadership Performance

You will never develop the true value of the business enterprise to its fullest potential until you get the people process right. In the previous chapter, I explained how behavior and critical thinking skills impact an individual's leadership ability. This chapter provides case studies from companies I have consulted with so you can see how these behaviors and critical thinking skills actually played out in the workplace in various leadership roles. When I work with client companies, our goal is always to ensure the right people are placed in the right roles where they can thrive and fulfill their greatest potential.

You'll read accounts of both successes and failures in a variety of positions. The names and details in the case studies have been changed to protect the privacy of the individuals and the companies involved. In each case study there will be a graph that represents the composite of all the assessments that were administered, along with the raw scores from all of the assessments, so you can see how the scores are interconnected. This will give you some insight into the details of how assessments work. I, myself, find it fascinating how the combinations of assessments and relevant scores have such revealing properties. Hopefully, you will gain an understanding and an appreciation of the process—how much assessments reveal and how they support the process of identifying and developing your leaders. The combinations of factors you are about to read in the case studies regarding the 16PF Questionnaire are further supported in Dr. Michael Karson's book, *16PF in Clinical Practice;* and Dr. James Schuerger and Dr. Heather Cattell's book, *Essentials of 16PF Assessments;* and Wendy Lord's two books, *Personality in Practice* and *Overcoming Obstacles to Interpretation,* as well as over 2,000 published articles on the 16PF Questionnaire.

Presented here are seven case studies from various client assignments. In an attempt to bring you real-life scenarios and to share the good and the bad, the first five will examine experiences of a series of failed managers and executives to help you see how critical it is to assess your leadership talent. The last two will show you the kinds of traits that are indicative of strong leaders. The raw scores from the various assessments are condensed into what we call our Profile Summary Graph (PSG), which is the summary of the assessment scores used to analyze the traits an individual possesses. There will be a PSG that accompanies each case study so you can see the data that is obtained from the various assessments and how the data is used collectively. To set the stage for each case study, I will present a brief background of the individual and the position, the circumstances, our interpretation of the results, and our recommendations. This information will be presented first, then the PSG, and then, immediately after the PSG, I will provide an analysis of the results and their relevance to the information we used to explain our findings and the combinations of scores and their meanings.

You will see how using multiple assessments gives greater meaning to the interpretation but, more importantly, you will see the depth of the 16PF Questionnaire because of its ability to look at the combinations of factors that will identify the behavioral patterns I referred to in the last chapter. It is significant to mention here that every assessment on the market will generate some type of computer-generated report, but in this process the only way a report can be generated is from a custom, written report. It is impossible to create a computer-generated report when you are using multiple assessments to compare and contrast results.

As I have stressed, it becomes difficult, if not impossible, to use just one assessment when you are trying to determine the depth of a person's strengths and weaknesses and potential for success. When you use a battery of assessments you are using what is referred to as *multiple factor analysis*. This allows you to see the many facets and traits of an individual because the different assessments give you varying perspectives regarding both personal attributes and critical thinking skills. The significance of using a battery of assessments is that the overall data allows you to focus in on the traits the individual possesses with greater certainty. Using a battery of assessments provides a result that clarifies whether certain traits and personality characteristics may or may not be problematic. Using a battery of assessments allows us to not only see the potential strengths but see the potential concerns or issues ahead of the hire or promotion. More importantly, as you build your pipeline and create your succession plans, you will have deeper insight into the individual's full potential. In addition, you will be able to craft and customize an in-depth development plan and identify the person's ability as a high-potential prospect.

The case studies will show you the power of the assessments and their predictive value from many different perspectives. The last two case studies will allow you to compare and contrast the first five and enable you to see the differences in behaviors and critical thinking skills that separate those who have struggled in their roles and those who have succeeded.

Case Study #1: Quality Control Manager Pre-Hire Assessment

Background

As you try to fill key positions and build your management team through external hires, the use of assessments can help distinguish between a good hire and a marginal hire or a bad hire. This first case study is an example of how this works. It is about an individual who was applying for the role of quality manager for one of our clients in its manufacturing facility. The previous quality manager was promoted to be plant manager, which created this opening. Obviously, you want to build a strong pipeline as you bring on new and talented people and look toward the future. You want to hire the best and the brightest so that you have the talent to promote from within. Making the wrong choice may result in a bad fit and derail the pipeline process so you have to get this part right.

Throughout the hiring and screening process, everything about this individual looked positive and the company was looking to make an offer and to hire him. His résumé supported his experience and credentials. Observations throughout the entire interview process suggested he was a viable candidate. Everyone who interviewed him had a favorable impression. Fortunately, this company does its due diligence and has a unique process in place to help eliminate hiring mistakes. The typical pattern during the hiring process for most companies is that once people pass the interviewing stage and everybody likes them, they get hired. Any further investigation stops because everyone agreed they liked the candidate. Once they get hired it's too late and it's usually about three to six months down the road before the hiring manager finds out something was missed.

Since everything seemed appropriate and the candidate came across so well, he was given an opportunity to come in and spend several days in the plant. This way the individual could explore the processes and understand the methodology in which the company operated and the organization could also gain some insight into this person's level of knowledge and whether he was a potential fit. This individual was given a few small assignments within the plant as part of a trial basis before a formal offer was made. During this time, the initial observations were favorable and the organization liked what it saw, which warranted further exploration into offering this individual the role. There were no red flags up to this point. While the organization began to check references, the company asked me to evaluate the individual's behaviors and capabilities and put him through our battery of assessments. After administering the assessments, the results from his critical thinking tests suggested that this individual possessed below average critical thinking skills and below average problem solving abilities and would have a difficult time making sound, stable judgments and decisions.

The assessments evaluating his critical thinking skills showed results of someone who is more of a hands-on learner and a concrete thinker and not a very strong problem solver. Additionally, his test scores raised concerns he was not likely to be able to think outside the box or think in abstract terms, both of which were necessary for the position. If you're administering just one critical thinking skills test, you may be inclined to speculate that someone may not be good at test taking, but when all of the assessment results turn out low there is cause for concern. This is just one of the values of using multiple assessments.

His assessment results suggested it wasn't just his critical thinking skills that were a concern; there were also significant concerns about his personality and the behaviors that were present in his assessment results. The results further suggested a heightened level of overly dominant tendencies and even a high probability he possessed overly assertive tendencies. Competitive and confident behaviors play an essential part in management but when they are too extreme and not kept in check while managing others, these behaviors are going to negatively impact morale at some point. Furthermore, the results suggested those aggressive tendencies could spill over into some underlying anger issues. His aggressive tendencies, coupled with the concerns that he possessed poorer decision-making skills, showed that he had qualities that wouldn't be valued in this role. The results also suggested that he saw himself as a perfectionist and didn't see himself as someone who made mistakes. Trait scores also suggested there was a strong possibility he was lacking in self-insight. Other scores suggested not only an argumentative demeanor but someone who possessed an overly strong ego. In other words, he had an overly inflated opinion of himself and his ego was likely to be too overbearing.

While conducting the reference check, the company found out the individual had a grievance over compensation with a previous employer. The individual felt that the compensation was unjust and in retaliation he damaged company property. You can't make this up! Seriously, this behavior does happen. When you hear about it, you have to ask, "What kind of an individual would resort to such measures?" and "Can assessment results really pick these behaviors out ahead of time?" The answer again is yes, but not all assessments are far reaching enough to do so, as I have explained.

In conjunction with his overall assessment scores, the behaviors that were revealed through further research are not surprising. That is because the scores from his profile reflect someone who is argumentative and strongly opinionated in his belief that he justifies his own actions. In other words, he is more forgiving of his own faults than he is of others and, in turn, believes his own actions are justified. Other scores suggest he is not very sound in his decision making which played out when, as a means of revenge and getting even, he damaged company property. This incident is not surprising given his overall assessment scores. Here are the assessment results that provided these insights into his behaviors.

Analysis
To evaluate this candidate, four assessments were administered. For higher-level positions we use as many as six different assessments, as we base the number of assessments on the level and complexity of the role. We used two that measure personality and behavior using the 16PF Questionnaire and the DiSC. These are used to support and confirm certain traits and behavioral patterns. In addition, we used two assessments that measure critical thinking skills. This is how we were able to assess his abilities and

potential concerns ahead of time. His critical thinking, problem-solving, and decision-making skills were evaluated using two different assessments, but we were able to further substantiate his thinking skills in a third way because the 16PF Questionnaire has a short problem-solving component as well. Using all these assessments is a way to ensure we evaluate several types of problem-solving ability and not simply take for granted he is strong or weak in this area.

He was given a perceptual reasoning test. (See symbol CF, which stands for "Culture Fair," at the bottom of the graph/CF 83). This is a test that measures nonverbal reasoning and is not affected by education, culture, or gender. It is a test that measures fluid intelligence and is a true IQ test. It measures a person's perceptual reasoning through the use of diagrams and spatial relationships, not words. His perceptual reasoning score was well below normal. A range of 90 to 110 is average; the mean score for this scale is 100. With a CF score of 83, he is seventeen points below the mean, which is indicative of people who are slow, methodical learners. The next assessment he took measured his cognitive reasoning ability; he also scored extremely low on this assessment. It has 126 questions, alternating between language and quantitative questions. On his linguistic (L), his raw score was a 25, placing him in the fourth percentile and his quantitative (Q) raw score was 18 placing him in the third percentile, which were both significantly below average. His overall scores placed him in the bottom second percentile when comparing his scores to management norms. This assessment helps measure an individual's ability to learn skills quickly, adjust to new situations, understand complex or subtle relationships, and think flexibly. Research shows a strong relationship between general mental ability and various work-related outcomes. These low scores usually manifest themselves in an inability to communicate clearly, most likely in written form, but his verbal communication scores indicated that he may be challenged in this area.

We use several assessments to gain a deeper understanding of a person's problem-solving and creative thinking skills and low scores on all assessments signify potential problems. The third data point relevant to his problem-solving ability is evident in his 16PF scores, where his low reasoning ability from his "B" score of 2 is also of significant concern. Statistically speaking, you can guess and obtain a score of 3 on this scale. There are fifteen problems written at a fifth-grade reading level that are math and word-related problems that he had trouble answering. All three of his assessment results related to his problem-solving ability are well below average and indicative of a person who is likely a concrete thinker and a hands-on, visual learner. Here you have three different assessments that measure various types of problem-solving ability that all correlate with lower than average reasoning and problem-solving ability. For someone seeking the position of quality manager, these scores raise significant concerns about whether he has the skill set to be an effective problem solver and decision maker. The references we received confirmed our concerns around his poor decision-making ability. This played out when he resorted to damaging company property to get even. This is not normal behavior, nor is it a well-thought-out, rational course of action.

In looking at his results from his personality and behavior assessments, additional areas of concern emerged that are indicative of someone who may not take a rational course of action. As we look at scores from his 16PF Questionnaire, we can assume he has an overly aggressive demeanor with the E9 (Assertive) and L7 (Suspicion) scores. The problem is the combination of these two traits line up to reveal that this person potentially has an extremely aggressive personality that is prone to challenge people, often in unproductive ways. These two scores also have a high correlation to anger-related personality traits. In this example we have added the DiSC assessment to see if there are any correlating scores that support his behavioral tendencies. His higher than average D (Dominance/DiSC) score, which remains high in both graphs, gives us confirmation of his need for dominance over others. In the second graph, the "I" (Influencing) drops substantially from the fourth segment to first segment. This can be identified by the numbered segments listed on the right side of the graphs. This shift is significant and concerning, as it suggests he can have a very direct style under pressure. His 16PF traits align with the DiSC scores and suggest a high probability that he has arrogant tendencies with his scores of E9 (Assertive), H9 (Socially Bold), and O3 (Unconcerned). He is likely to believe that whatever he does is perfect, according to his scores of E9 (Assertive, Confidence), G7 (Rule Conscious), Q3/8 (Perfectionist), and O3 (Unconcerned). His scores of H9 (Socially Bold), and O3 (Unconcerned) suggest he is more forgiving of himself and his shortcomings than others and tends to not look back or second guess what he has done.

If you were to look at his DiSC scores alone, he seems like a relatively good candidate. His DiSC results suggest he is a task-driven, no-nonsense sort of individual which, for a quality manager, is not a bad thing. However, as I have mentioned before, the DiSC is not strong enough to be used as a selection tool on its own because it does not measure behavior deeply enough and it does not measure problem-solving ability. Still, it works as a supporting tool to help piece together the traits that someone is likely to have. The real value of using multiple-factor analysis is the ability to see confirming data from various angles that support the results.

Imagine if the organization decided to hire this person on face value from the resume and interview! This happens all too often. Some companies believe you can use the DiSC as a hiring tool and, in fact, do. As I've said, I stress that the DiSC is not supported as a selection tool from the publisher. In this example, if a company was using the DiSC as a selection tool, along with the positive interview that was conducted, this candidate would have been hired. As we have seen, the DiSC does not sort out the more problematic behaviors, but it does confirm some of the behaviors that are concerning.

What if the organization had not been able to ascertain the information from the references? What if it had not used some type of an assessment process to uncover any challenges? The odds are in his favor that he would likely have been hired. He passed the interview and his trial days in the plant went well. This example shows that not only must you check references but you must utilize the appropriate assessments when selecting candidates for key roles.

There are several dynamics at play here. When a candidate passes the interview process in relatively strong fashion because everyone who has interviewed the candidate likes the person, he or she usually gets hired. Often, it can be difficult to get valuable or real data when you check references. Another dynamic lies in the fact that many organizations do not use assessments. Of those who do, the vast majority will not use an assessment to eliminate a candidate. However, here you can clearly see based on the assessment results why our recommendation to the client was to find a more appropriate candidate and why this person shouldn't be hired. The overall test results suggested this would be more than just a poor fit: it would be a bad hire. Because of his past experience and knowledge he was well into the interview and hiring process before any of his flaws and issues were detected. In fact, this happens all too frequently. On the other hand, a well-designed and well-constructed battery of assessments is harder to get past.

The Executive Group
Profile Summary Graph (PSG)

Case Study #1   **B. Sample**

Pre-Hire Assessment   **Quality Manager**

PRIMARY PERSONALITY FACTORS   IM **16**   IN **O**   AQ **54**

Factor	Sten	Left Meaning	Standard Ten Score (STEN) 1 2 3 4 5 6 7 8 9 10	Right Meaning
A	5	RESERVED Unengaging, Distant	• (5)	SOCIABLE Engaging, friendly
B	2	CONCRETE THINKING Hands on learning	• (2)	ABSTRACT THINKING Independent learning
C	8	EASILY UPSET Job should fit needs	• (8)	MANAGES FRUSTRATION Can adapt to job
E	9	SUBMISSIVE More passive, humble	• (9)	ASSERTIVE Competitive, confident
F	3	SERIOUS Sober, somber	• (3)	ENTHUSIASTIC Happy, lively, energetic
G	7	UNCONVENTIONAL Ignores expectations	• (7)	CONVENTIONAL Follows rules
H	9	SOCIALLY RESTRAINED Shy, avoids spotlight	• (9)	SOCIALLY BOLD Needs to impress others
I	4	TOUGH-MINDED Realistic, no-nonsense	• (4)	SENSITIVE Susceptible to feelings
L	7	TRUSTING Accepting, naïve	• (7)	SUSPICIOUS Skeptical, blaming
M	5	PRACTICAL Focus on solutions	• (5)	IMPRACTICAL Focus on ideas
N	6	DIRECT WITH OTHERS Self-disclosing, open	• (6)	INDIRECT WITH OTHERS Discreet, diplomatic, private
O	3	UNCONCERNED Casual, untroubled	• (3)	WORRYING Fear of mistakes
Q1	5	RESISTS CHANGE Prefers the familiar	• (5)	OPEN TO CHANGE Experimenting
Q2	3	WORKS IN GROUPS Collaborative	• (3)	WORKS ALONE Independent, self-reliant
Q3	8	LESS ORDERLY Can be undisciplined	• (8)	MORE ORDERLY Perfectionistic
Q4	2	PATIENT Relaxed, calm	• (2)	IMPATIENT Tense, driven

GRAPH I	GRAPH II
D I S C	D I S C
6 4 1 7	6 1 5 4
CREATIVE	ACHIEVER

Reasoning/Problem Solving   Global Factors

Raw Scores	Percentiles	
		EX __6__
L __25__	__4__ %	ER __3__
Q __18__	__3__ %	TM __7__
T __43__	__2__ %	IN __9__
Norms Used - **MGR**		SC __8__
cr __83__	__14__ %	__3__ Sten
WG ____	____ %	
Norms Used - ____		

Case Study 12.1 Pre-Hire Assessment[6]

---

[6]   16PF Profile adapted with permission from the Institute for Personality and Ability Testing, Inc. (2009). 16PF Fifth Edition Questionnaire Manual. Savoy, IL.

Case Study # 2: Operations Manager
Internal Promotion

Background

This next case study discusses how assessments were used as part of evaluating an internal employee being considered for promotion into a management role. She was very talented and dedicated but not without her challenges. The organization was considering her for a promotion because of her strong skill sets, but there were concerns about her demeanor as her behavior and attitude were problematic more often than not. Our recommendation was not to promote her. Additionally, we recommended that the organization consider placing her on a PIP. The inappropriate behavior she displayed usually went unchecked. It was overlooked because of her solid work output. However, since the bad behavior was never addressed, she continued to repeat these actions.

This was an individual who had aspirations of being promoted into management. She was an extremely smart and capable hard worker who could outperform two of her peers in customer service. She went above and beyond her duties to help write the technical manuals and assisted the plant in getting its ISO accreditation. She was very competent and knew a tremendous amount about how the organization operated and its workflow because of her longevity at the organization. However, no one wanted to work with her. Her peers and others she worked with had little tolerance for her. Not only was she good at what she did, she was intelligent and had strong problem-solving and critical thinking skills to match her technical skills. Her perceptual reasoning score on her IQ test was 118, eighteen points above the mean, placing her in the above-average range. (Compare that to our first case study when that person scored an 83 on his perceptual reasoning test.) To provide perspective, 90–110 is average, with 100 as the mean. One hundred and ten to 120 is above average, and 120–140 is superior. Her perceptual reasoning was well above average at 118. Her linguistic and quantitative skills were in the seventieth percentile overall, suggesting someone who was well read, intelligent, and a quick learner. It is not surprising that she helped write the ISO manuals and led the ISO compliance initiative in this organization. She was hard working and competitively driven, as was evident in her work and confirmed by her assessment scores. Her aspirations to get into management were of no surprise.

Her assessment scores show someone who is extremely competitive but also someone who would be considered highly aggressive, as certain scores were elevated and in the extreme direction. Furthermore, we also see tendencies of someone who can be argumentative and angry. Her scores suggest a lack of emotional resolve and stability and an inability to manage stress. All these tendencies would collide with each other and the behaviors were likely to exacerbate when she was in an argumentative state. Often her emotions got the best of her; she tended to argue with people, tell others what to do, talk down to colleagues, get upset quickly, and alienate many of the people she worked with. It was not unusual to see her talk "at" people and "down" to people instead of "to" them. While she was highly respected for her knowledge, contribution, and work ethic within the organization, people tolerated her but distanced themselves, not wanting to work with her or even be around her.

She sought to grow into a management role. The owner wanted to give her an opportunity and believed that if she were to be promoted, these tendencies would diminish and her overall demeanor might settle down if she finally achieved her goal. He felt that rewarding her because of her hard work and dedication might help her mature enough to grow professionally. We disagreed, noting that these traits were so extreme that these behaviors would not moderate if she were in a leadership role. In spite of our recommendations, the owner wanted to give her a chance and she was promoted to oversee three functional areas of operations. Within six months she was terminated. Here are her results, why we expressed concerns, and why our predictions played out so accurately.

Analysis

We used the same four assessments for this person that we used for the Quality Manger in the first case study. It's easy to see her competitive, results-driven, get-it-done mentality from her DiSC scores. Both graphs are relatively the same, indicating this is a fair representation of her. Her dominance in her DiSC scores, which is the high D in the seventh segment, sustains the high D profile in the second graph. This correlates to the high E9 (Assertive) on her 16PF Questionnaire. What the 16PF Questionnaire picks out—that the DiSC cannot—is the aggressiveness that accompanies her dominance with her L9 (Suspicion). We know that the combination of E9 (Assertive) and L9 (Suspicion) denotes anger, aggression, and argumentative tendencies. These are behaviors that emerged in her interactions with others.

Further evaluation shows she cannot manage stress and has fewer coping skills, which is revealed in her score of ER 7 (Emotional Resilience; One of the Global Scales that are part of the Big 5 Theory mentioned in chapter 6) and was also witnessed regularly. We can discern this from her Global Scales on Emotional Resilience as it is higher than normal at 7. Normal range is 4. Further we see she can't control her anger when upset from her ER7 (Emotional Resilience), C3 (Easily Upset), and L7 (Suspicion). These scores suggest that she becomes confrontational, has a short fuse, and does not bounce back quickly from stressful or challenging situations. These were the same behaviors that were often witnessed and played out in her interactions with others. Another combination of scores of L9 (Suspicion), F4 (Serious/Somber), and O5 (Worry/Self-Doubt) suggests she can't find any humor or levity to offset her anger.

As we look further we see her tendencies to talk down to others because she sees herself as smarter than them and does not trust that others can keep up with her; her impatience shows through. These scores come from her IQ of 118, along with her cognitive reasoning scores being high (seventieth percentile) and her need to dominate others, which is her high D from her DiSC and her E9 (Assertive), both suggesting the need to have the last word, tell others what to do, and be in charge. It is interesting to note that all these traits were also the drivers pushing her to be in a managerial role.

The overall scores presented in her assessments suggest this is someone who has a hard time accepting criticism, gets emotional quickly, and becomes argumentative and confrontational rapidly. All this, coupled with her strong intellectual ability, creates a sense of intellectualized hostility, which is part of her personality makeup. Overcoming these issues would require far more assistance than a business coach or a behavioral coach could provide; she would probably benefit from other counseling. The owner's desire to see if this employee could change once promoted is admirable. However, the problematic behaviors revealed by her assessment results suggested she was not going to change, and the behaviors would only elevate once she was in a position of power, which she ultimately overused, as we predicted. We weren't surprised that she was terminated in six short months after her promotion.

This is another example of what a battery of assessments can reveal about an individual and their tendencies. Unfortunately, many companies, as in this case, choose not to adhere to the findings from the assessments. The tendency is to focus on longevity and other skills that are needed to succeed in a role and as is common, ignore what the assessment results reveal. This particular case study further supports the theory that behavior is a better predictor of performance than skills, abilities, and even intelligence. Here is the interesting and most telling piece: After being fired, she went on to get hired by two other companies and was fired from both of them as well over the next three years. She has continued to get hired because of her job knowledge, talents, and skills but then is fired for her behavior and attitude. No one can deny that her knowledge and skills are quite impressive, but the battery of assessments predicted her behaviors would be too much to overcome and eventually cause her downfall. In this case we were able to predict the outcome ahead of time, which speaks to the power of the assessment process when used properly.

The Executive Group
Profile Summary Graph (PSG)

Case Study #2
Internal Promotion

M. Sample
Operations Manager

PRIMARY PERSONALITY FACTORS   IM **8**   IN **0**   AQ **63**

Factor	Sten	Left Meaning	Standard Ten Score (STEN) 1–10	Right Meaning
A	5	RESERVED Unengaging, Distant	• (5)	SOCIABLE Engaging, friendly
B	8	CONCRETE THINKING Hands on learning	• (8)	ABSTRACT THINKING Independent learning
C	3	EASILY UPSET Job should fit needs	• (3)	MANAGES FRUSTRATION Can adapt to job
E	9	SUBMISSIVE More passive, humble	• (9)	ASSERTIVE Competitive, confident
F	4	SERIOUS Sober, somber	• (4)	ENTHUSIASTIC Happy, lively, energetic
G	6	UNCONVENTIONAL Ignores expectations	• (6)	CONVENTIONAL Follows rules
H	5	SOCIALLY RESTRAINED Shy, avoids spotlight	• (5)	SOCIALLY BOLD Needs to impress others
I	5	TOUGH-MINDED Realistic, no-nonsense	• (5)	SENSITIVE Susceptible to feelings
L	9	TRUSTING Accepting, naïve	• (9)	SUSPICIOUS Skeptical, blaming
M	4	PRACTICAL Focus on solutions	• (4)	IMPRACTICAL Focus on ideas
N	5	DIRECT WITH OTHERS Self-disclosing, open	• (5)	INDIRECT WITH OTHERS Discreet, diplomatic, private
O	5	UNCONCERNED Casual, untroubled	• (5)	WORRYING Fear of mistakes
Q1	5	RESISTS CHANGE Prefers the familiar	• (5)	OPEN TO CHANGE Experimenting
Q2	5	WORKS IN GROUPS Collaborative	• (5)	WORKS ALONE Independent, self-reliant
Q3	5	LESS ORDERLY Can be undisciplined	• (5)	MORE ORDERLY Perfectionistic
Q4	5	PATIENT Relaxed, calm	• (5)	IMPATIENT Tense, driven

GRAPH I	GRAPH II
D I S C	D I S C
DEVELOPER	DEVELOPER
7 2 1 4	7 2 3 3

Reasoning/Problem Solving   **Global Factors**

Raw Scores	Percentiles		
L **43**	**67** %	EX	**5**
Q **32**	**70** %	ER	**7**
T **75**	**70** %	TM	**7**
Norms Used - **T/S**		IN	**8**
CF **118**	**87** %	SC	**6**
WG ___	___ %		**8** Sten

Norms Used - ____

Case Study 12.2 Internal Promotion[7]

---

[7]   16PF Profile adapted with permission from the Institute for Personality and Ability Testing, Inc. (2009). 16PF Fifth Edition Questionnaire Manual. Savoy, IL.

Case Study #3: VP of Sales
Performance Coaching Assignment

Background

This case study shows how we are guilty of taking a talented high performer and making him a manager when we could have predicted ahead of time this particular role would not be a good match. This was an internal individual who had already been promoted from a successful stint as a salesman to the position of vice president of sales. His performance as a salesperson was outstanding, as this individual was well suited in a role as an individual contributor. However, his performance as the vice president was dismal at best, and the organization wanted to provide coaching to see if he could be helped.

This man is one of the nicest, most sincere, and conscientious individuals you would ever want to meet; you would love to have him as a friend and neighbor. He is truly a gentleman and a very dedicated individual but, unfortunately, he was in the wrong role. You may be wondering how this individual could be in the wrong position if he is so nice and had a strong track record. As I began the coaching process, working on various aspects related to his gaps, and as more pressure was being placed on him by the organization for sales results, he resigned. He came to his own realization that he was not cut out for management and left voluntarily. When this kind of situation happens everyone loses. Unfortunately, we lose a good salesperson, a dedicated company man and we expend time, money, and energy to promote someone. However, we could have predicted the outcome in advance.

After reviewing his assessment results, his sales results, the expectations, and his skills and abilities, I had expressed concerns to upper management that this individual was in over his head and that this was not likely going to be a success story because his personality did not fit the role. While my role as a coach is to help an individual work through the developmental initiatives to get through to the other side, I have to be aware of whether or not the individual can achieve sustainable results as an outcome of the coaching and development process or whether we are just placing a Band-Aid on the wound. The question becomes whether this person gets to where he needs to be and how long it will take. In this case the individual opted out when the pressure began to mount. Here is a situation where the assessment results reveal an individual who has many positive skills, behaviors, and attributes but not the kind of personality to drive the desired sales results in a sales management role. I will walk through the personality traits that show why he was struggling in the position and will also show why this promotion set him up for failure and how the organization, while well-intentioned, did him an injustice and, in the end, lost a valuable employee.

Analysis
His sales results as an individual contributor were above average. They were above average because he is

conscientious, smart, analytical, and intuitive, and has a good sense of self-discipline. He possesses an awareness of others and places the needs of others above his own. I refer to his 16PF profile as the "good soldier" profile. In addition, he has an easygoing demeanor with the desire to help and take care of others, and he loves to analyze data. His style is not one that is gregarious, outgoing, energetic, and highly driven to succeed by driving results through others. While he was successful as a salesperson, he did so because he had a low-key, methodical, and calculating style. He does not operate with a high sense of urgency but prides himself on being consistent.

There is a striking similarity as you look at his 16PF scores and his DiSC scores, including both DiSC graphs. Both assessments represent an individual who is cautious, conservative, nondemonstrative, and conflict-avoidant. These are not typical behavioral traits of someone who is expected to drive sales results through others. In essence, he is uncomfortable in a role that requires directing the efforts of others. As we analyze his 16PF profile, it is one we refer to as shapeless. There are not a lot of defining behavioral traits that stand out as all of his scores are pretty much down the middle. As a general rule we know people with this profile tend to be a great team player, loyal and conscientious, but this pattern does not match that of someone who is driven to manage others. Furthermore, his DiSC scores reveal someone who is less demonstrative and assertive with his lower D (Dominance). It is below the midline and this lower level of dominance shows that he does not like to take a dominant lead. His DiSC pattern sustains that same pattern in both graphs suggesting consistency in behavior. This provides further validation between both DiSC graphs and the flatness of his 16PF profile.

This individual was a former high school math teacher. His background shows up in his much higher quantitative (Q) raw score of 42 placing him in the eighty-sixth percentile on his cognitive reasoning test. His perceptual reasoning (IQ) CF 109 pushes the upper end of average, as 110 to 120 is considered above average for natural intelligence. His problem-solving score on his 16PF Questionnaire was an 8, and the sum total of all three of his critical thinking skills tests shows him to have the intellectual capabilities to manage such a role. He would spend hours evaluating market data, territory analysis, advertising results, sales numbers, and call reports but never leave the office.

He had regular sales meetings but never went on sales calls with his staff. He was excellent at reporting the obvious. The role of market analyst would be a much better fit than the spot as vice president of sales. He loved the analysis and strategy planning, but doesn't like to challenge others and does not like conflict. He was well liked by everyone but he did not like to manage and direct others. Similar situations when someone is promoted happen frequently and again show the predictive value of assessments whether you are hiring, promoting, or coaching someone. There were developmental initiatives put into place as the coaching engagement evolved but, in time, he realized on his own that he was better off in a role as an individual contributor than a manager and chose to leave the company. The unfortunate end was the company lost a great salesperson because they lacked the ability to assess his full capabilities ahead of time. This is another example of how utilizing assessments in the selection or promotion process can help shed more light on an individual's character and potential for success.

The Executive Group
Profile Summary Graph (PSG)

Case Study #3 | D. Sample
Performance Coaching Assignment | VP Sales

PRIMARY PERSONALITY FACTORS IM **8** IN **0** AQ **56**

Factor	Sten	Left Meaning	Standard Ten Score (STEN) 1–10	Right Meaning
A	6	RESERVED Unengaging, Distant	● (6)	SOCIABLE Engaging, friendly
B	8	CONCRETE THINKING Hands on learning	● (8)	ABSTRACT THINKING Independent learning
C	5	EASILY UPSET Job should fit needs	● (4)	MANAGES FRUSTRATION Can adapt to job
E	6	SUBMISSIVE More passive, humble	● (6)	ASSERTIVE Competitive, confident
F	5	SERIOUS Sober, somber	● (4)	ENTHUSIASTIC Happy, lively, energetic
G	6	UNCONVENTIONAL Ignores expectations	● (6)	CONVENTIONAL Follows rules
H	5	SOCIALLY RESTRAINED Shy, avoids spotlight	● (4)	SOCIALLY BOLD Needs to impress others
I	5	TOUGH-MINDED Realistic, no-nonsense	● (4)	SENSITIVE Susceptible to feelings
L	5	TRUSTING Accepting, naive	● (4)	SUSPICIOUS Skeptical, blaming
M	4	PRACTICAL Focus on solutions	● (3)	IMPRACTICAL Focus on ideas
N	5	DIRECT WITH OTHERS Self-disclosing, open	● (4)	INDIRECT WITH OTHERS Discreet, diplomatic, private
O	4	UNCONCERNED Casual, untroubled	● (3)	WORRYING Fear of mistakes
Q1	7	RESISTS CHANGE Prefers the familiar	● (7)	OPEN TO CHANGE Experimenting
Q2	6	WORKS IN GROUPS Collaborative	● (6)	WORKS ALONE Independent, self-reliant
Q3	5	LESS ORDERLY Can be undisciplined	● (4)	MORE ORDERLY Perfectionistic
Q4	4	PATIENT Relaxed, calm	● (3)	IMPATIENT Tense, driven

GRAPH I — D I S C — OBJECTIVE THINKER — 4 3 4 7

GRAPH II — D I S C — OBJECTIVE THINKER — 3 2 4 6

Reasoning/Problem Solving — Global Factors

	Raw Scores	Percentiles
L	40	40 %
Q	42	86 %
T	82	65 %

Norms Used - **MGR**

CF **109** 72 %

WG ___ ___%

Norms Used - ___

EX ___**5**___
ER ___**4**___
TM ___**5**___
IN ___**6**___
SC ___**6**___
___**7**___ Sten

Case Study 12.3 Performance Coaching Assignment[8]

---

[8] 16PF Profile adapted with permission from the Institute for Personality and Ability Testing, Inc. (2009). 16PF Fifth Edition Questionnaire Manual. Savoy, IL.

Case Study #4: VP of International Operations Intervention

Background

The previous case study involved efforts to help someone get to the next level and improve the areas in which he was underperforming. This case study is also about an existing manager, but this situation could not simply be addressed by coaching since there were much deeper issues. I was brought in to conduct an intervention because of overriding concerns the company had the wrong person in the role and it was trying to determine what to do next. The concern was whether this individual was going to be able to overcome her challenges. This intervention was an effort to see if this executive and the situation could be salvaged. This individual held an international role as vice president of operations for a $2 billion global manufacturer in the automotive sector as an OEM and aftermarket supplier. The operations she oversaw produced 60 percent of worldwide production. She was brought in because of her background and experience working for one of the Big 3. She was also chosen because of her automotive background and cultural fit. They did not conduct any kind of behavioral analysis pre-hire.

Her role was to oversee two plants, twenty miles apart, outside the United States. The plants operated 24/7 and had nearly 2,800 employees between both facilities. In her first fourteen months on the job, the two plants combined lost $1.1 million in operating costs. A 360 was conducted and revealed that her staff saw her as more unstable and demanding. She was actually labeled by people in her 360 review as "Attila the Hun," named after the fierce warrior and king of the horse-riding Huns who harassed the Roman Empire during the fifth century AD and put fear in people throughout the land.

I was brought in to conduct an intervention to see if the situation could be salvaged and if she could be helped. She was into year one of a two-year contract and the organization needed to know if it should buy her out of the contract or whether her behavior could be modified and turned around. With a hefty salary and the first-year losses, the concern came down to whether the issues could be worked through and, if so, how long it would take. If they couldn't be addressed, another plan would be needed. She was flown into the corporate offices to meet with me for the day and go through the interview, assessments, and evaluation process. Within the first hour of interaction and discussions around her current situation, and discussions about her 360 results and assessment results, she showed to be extremely distraught and got overly emotional about her failure and wasn't sure how it happened, how she got there, or how to change it.

In evaluating her assessment results from her 16PF Questionnaire, she is seen as someone who is kind, caring, sympathetic, nurturing, as well as people and relationship oriented. However, while she possesses these traits, she also showed an extremely low level of emotional resolve, someone who did not manage stress very well, and did not like conflict. Her DiSC results portrayed a confident person and showed her to be results driven, no-nonsense, unemotional, assertive, spontaneous, and aggressive. The interesting dynamic is that these two assessments are completely different in that one shows more of an emotional servant leader, while the other one shows her to be a very assertive leader. Here is a case in which we see where the differences between the two instruments give us deeper insight. Her DiSC and her 16PF results present two different people. The stress of the job and the dynamics of the manufacturing environment with several thousand employees in two locations created challenges that were too great for her to overcome. She subsequently lost control of the situation and production. With a strong automotive background, and solid experience in previous positions, as well as a strong cultural fit, it was assumed she would be able to bring about the needed change in the operations, but her lack of performance and improvement ultimately resulted in termination. Between her first-year salary and buying out the second year of her contract, along with losses in productivity and production, the organization had to take a $1.5 million loss.

As we look at her assessment results, we see that her critical thinking skills were in question, in relation to her ability to handle a role of this size and magnitude. In evaluating her 16 PF results, I had to question her emotional resolve and stability in managing her position. She became someone other than who she truly was in order to manage the operation. This ultimately led to her failure and was a major financial hardship for the organization.

Analysis

She is a driver of change with her Q1/10 (Open to Change) and this was supposedly a hallmark of her success in a prior role. She is kind-hearted and sensitive to people and their needs while, at the same time, she has an overly strong need to be liked. We can see this through her scores of A8 (Warmth), Q2/2 (Works in Groups/Group Dependent), and I8 (Sensitivity). Additional scores suggest she has a hard time holding people accountable and also has difficulty standing on her own and being able to make tough decisions. Again, we see this through her scores of E5 (Assertive), H6 (Socially Bold), O8 (Worry and Self-doubt), and Q2/2 (Works in Groups/Group Dependent).

Looking further at her 16PF scores we see she gets emotional and does not manage stressful situations with her global score of ER7 (Emotional Resilience). A normal score on this dimension is a 4, suggesting she may be prone to overreact. The scores impacting this are her C5 (Managing Frustration), L6 (Suspicion), O8 (Worry/Self-doubt), and Q4/5 (Impatience), all combining to reveal someone who does not manage pressure well. The combination of her I8 (Sensitivity) and her L6 (Suspicion) tells us she will lash out at others, and her O8 (Worry/Self-doubt) tells us she is not confident in her own abilities and she becomes overly critical of herself under pressure. She becomes overwhelmed quite quickly. The combination of her A8 (Warmth) and Q2/2 (Works in Groups/Group Dependent) tells us she has to have people around her; and her L6 (Suspicion) tells us she does not trust them; and her L6 (Suspicion), I8 (Sensitivity), and O8 (Worry/Self-doubt) tell us she will lash out, hence the "Attila the Hun" comments. In one breath she is their best friend and she wants them to like her, and in the next breath she is driving them away because she doesn't trust them. The lashing out emerges when she becomes stressed. An emotional state emerges from her being overly sensitive to criticism, which we see in her scores of I8 (Sensitivity) and O8 (Worry/Self-doubt). With an inability to withhold her thoughts, she is more prone to say what's bothering her up front with her N4 (Directness).

Several factors contributed to the organization buying out her contract: the financial losses from her division, her performance and behavior issues, and the feedback from her 360. The assessment process allowed the organization to see that her inherent characteristics were likely too insurmountable to be able to rectify in the immediate future, and the organization could not risk riding out one more year of her contract under these circumstances. These attributes never surfaced in her original interview, but they rarely ever do. With an apparently strong track record, experience in the automotive industry, and working with the Big 3, she seemed like the perfect fit. Her issues never surfaced in the references, and the organization did not use an assessment process for selection, so these traits went unnoticed until it was too late. This set the organization back financially and operationally for nearly thirty-six months. Again, here is another classic example of where the proper battery of assessments for such a high-level position could have circumvented a huge mistake yet instead it created a three-year setback. This is because it took another year to fill the position and stabilize operations.

The Executive Group
Profile Summary Graph (PSG)

Case Study #4   **P. Sample**

Intervention   **VP of International Operations**

PRIMARY PERSONALITY FACTORS   IM **12**   IN **0**   AQ **50**

Factor	Sten	Left Meaning	Standard Ten Score (STEN) 1–10	Right Meaning
A	8	RESERVED — Unengaging, Distant	● at 8	SOCIABLE — Engaging, friendly
B	6	CONCRETE THINKING — Hands on learning	● at 6	ABSTRACT THINKING — Independent learning
C	5	EASILY UPSET — Job should fit needs	● at 4	MANAGES FRUSTRATION — Can adapt to job
E	5	SUBMISSIVE — More passive, humble	● at 5	ASSERTIVE — Competitive, confident
F	6	SERIOUS — Sober, somber	● at 6	ENTHUSIASTIC — Happy, lively, energetic
G	5	UNCONVENTIONAL — Ignores expectations	● at 5	CONVENTIONAL — Follows rules
H	6	SOCIALLY RESTRAINED — Shy, avoids spotlight	● at 6	SOCIALLY BOLD — Needs to impress others
I	8	TOUGH-MINDED — Realistic, no-nonsense	● at 8	SENSITIVE — Susceptible to feelings
L	6	TRUSTING — Accepting, naive	● at 6	SUSPICIOUS — Skeptical, blaming
M	5	PRACTICAL — Focus on solutions	● at 5	IMPRACTICAL — Focus on ideas
N	4	DIRECT WITH OTHERS — Self-disclosing, open	● at 4	INDIRECT WITH OTHERS — Discreet, diplomatic, private
O	8	UNCONCERNED — Casual, untroubled	● at 8	WORRYING — Fear of mistakes
Q1	10	RESISTS CHANGE — Prefers the familiar	● at 10	OPEN TO CHANGE — Experimenting
Q2	2	WORKS IN GROUPS — Collaborative	● at 2	WORKS ALONE — Independent, self-reliant
Q3	4	LESS ORDERLY — Can be undisciplined	● at 4	MORE ORDERLY — Perfectionistic
Q4	5	PATIENT — Relaxed, calm	● at 5	IMPATIENT — Tense, driven

GRAPH I	GRAPH II
D I S C	D I S C
7 3 2 3	6 3 1 5
DEVELOPER	CREATIVE

Reasoning/Problem Solving

Raw Scores	Percentiles
L 32	14 %
Q 32	45 %
T 64	25 %

Norms Used - **MGR**

CF 109   72 %

WG ____ ____ %

Norms Used - ____

Global Factors

EX **8**

ER **7**

TM **2**

IN **7**

SC **5**

7 Sten

Case Study 12.4 Intervention[9]

---

[9] 16PF Profile adapted with permission from the Institute for Personality and Ability Testing, Inc. (2009). 16PF Fifth Edition Questionnaire Manual. Savoy, IL.

Case Study #5: Big East Engineering Grad with MBA Coaching/Intervention

Background

This is one of my most interesting case studies as you will come to see why, as the dynamics and assessment results unfold. I provide assessment results to another executive coach who specializes in cases where there are deep-seated personal and business issues challenging an individual. We have worked together for about thirteen years. He uses our assessments with his coaching cases and relies on our assessment process to help him see personality attributes of his clients so he can identify some of the underlying challenges he is faced with in his work with an individual. This helps him further measure the coaching and treatment part of his program and saves time in his analysis. In my chapter on coaching, I alluded to using the appropriate coach based on the dynamics and severity of the situation, and this is one of those cases.

This particular case had its challenges, including extreme behavioral issues that were impacting job performance and the ability to hold a job. This individual seemed to have all the attributes necessary for a successful career but, at a young age, he had already been fired twice. This unique case study will show the relevancy of how a well-designed set of assessments has a high level of ability to predict behavior, performance, and outcomes in the workplace ahead of time.

I was asked to provide the assessment data to support the coaching work of my colleague. My evaluation from the assessment results was confirmed by my colleague; as the findings from his assessments were the things that comprised much of this individual's challenges. After my evaluation I was asked to review the results with the individual in person along with the executive coach. The goal was to aid in the process to help create a personal and professional development plan based on the assessment results. His assessment results suggested he was a very smart individual with above-average intelligence and strong academic credentials. They also revealed that he might be less than genuine in his interactions and, furthermore, might resist any real efforts to change. Some people do turn their lives around in similar circumstances, but his assessment results indicated he had no realization of a need to change.

When I met him, I found an articulate, composed, and confident individual. He was tall with strikingly good looks, a professional presence, and a respectful demeanor, at least on the surface. During our time together, he said all the right things, including addressing the issues most important for him to work on for his success. What is critical to understand is that in a job setting, as interviewers, it is unlikely that we'll see past this façade. I observed that part of his personality he wanted me to see, which he capably projected and for the entire day, including through lunch. This is the kind of appropriate behavior you would expect to see in an interview when someone is trying to make a good impression and is intent on putting his best foot forward. However, I had the advantage of additional insight into his personality and behaviors that were revealed in his assessment results. His test results tell us a great deal about who he really is and why his work history, in only a few years out of college, is already storied.

As I have previously mentioned, there are situations when a more extensive battery of assessments is appropriate, and this was one of those times. Using additional assessments supported and validated all of the findings and enabled us to uncover these kinds of behavioral dynamics. In this instance, I added two more assessments from those used in the first few case studies; they include a Hogan report, which looks at stressors, and also an assessment that measures inductive and deductive reasoning and how someone logically works through problems.

Based on his assessment results, I recommended my colleague use extra caution with this engagement because the profile showed characteristics of someone who was undependable, unpredictable, prone to being untruthful, and had an extremely low level of discipline. Unfortunately, these concerns played out and, within three months of the coaching engagement, the person starting missing appointments and then began bouncing checks for services. Here are his assessment results and my findings:

Analysis

There are a number of dynamics at play here, and I will explain the combinations of scores and the interrelationship of all of the assessments. When I initially called my friend to provide a debriefing of the results, I knew nothing other than this individual's name and what the results were suggesting. Here is my analysis of what the assessment results revealed and why I told my colleague to be cautious in his dealings with this person.

While this individual is extremely intelligent, presents well, and says all the right things—E10 (Assertive), F8 (Enthusiastic), H9 (Socially Bold)—it is likely just a front, as he disguises himself well. Underneath he appears to be impulsive, unfettered, and carefree, with scores of F8 (Enthusiastic), M8 (Impractical), G4 (Unconventional) and Q3/1 (Undisciplined); someone who would buck authority and challenge the system: Q1/10 (Open to Change), L7 (Suspicion), and G4 (Unconventional). He can be defiant, flighty, and impulsive: E10 (Assertive), F8 (Enthusiastic), H9 (Socially Bold), G4 (Unconventional), L7 (Suspicion), M8 (Impractical), and Q1/10 (Open to Change). He does not seem to like to conform, appears to be undisciplined: G4 (Unconventional), and Q3/1 (Undisciplined); and is likely disrespectful when he is angry or does not get his way: E10 (Assertive), L7 Suspicion), G4 (Unconventional), and O3 (Unconcerned).

His assessment results also show traits of a well-entrenched ego with possible narcissist tendencies: E10

(Assertive), H9 (Socially Bold), and O3 (Unconcerned). He sees himself as better than, and smarter than, everyone else: E10 (Assertive), H9 (Socially Bold), L7 (Suspicion), O3 (Unconcerned), and B6 (Reasoning and Problem Solving). He is colorful and good at telling people what they want to hear while, at the same time, he can be verbally sarcastic in his tone: E10 (Assertive), F8 (Enthusiastic), H9 (Socially Bold), G4 (Unconventional), and L7 (Suspicion).

I evaluated combinations of scores from all of his assessment results to construct a picture of his tendencies. This is where using the predictive value of the 16PF Questionnaire is incredibly profound. When you add the Hogan and the DiSC, you get confirming patterns to his behavior. His L7 (Suspicion) correlates with his Skeptical scale on his Hogan report, which is identified as a high-risk area. There are four high-risk areas in total from his Hogan report, and you can track them back to the 16PF Questionnaire. Again, by using multiple assessments, we are able to look deeply into patterns of behavior and get a sense of how someone thinks and behaves. This level of insight can only be achieved through the use of an assessment battery.

My colleague confirmed that this behavior is what he had observed and indicated it was also what had been seen in this individual's work behavior. The information, along with the observations from my visit, supported what had evolved over the duration of the coaching assignment. I later learned that this individual dropped out of the coaching sessions with my colleague, believing he was fine and didn't need help. His scores suggest that he doesn't like to conform to the structured meetings and sessions required in order for him to make positive changes. His ego and rebellious side are most likely getting in his way.

I include this case study as it has an extremely high relevance to the selection process. This case study epitomizes what happens during the interview process as it demonstrates how highly intelligent and skilled people can do well in an interview and portray themselves as capable when, in fact, they will create problems in the workplace because they have challenges they have not worked through. It is no wonder two different firms have hired this young man and it's no surprise that both of these firms terminated this young man. Again, I'm stressing that assessments are an important part of the discovery process when evaluating talent and they should be included in the selection and leadership development process.

The Executive Group
Profile Summary Graph (PSG)

Case Study #5

J. Sample

Intervention/Coaching

Big East Engineering Grad with MBA

PRIMARY PERSONALITY FACTORS   IM **5**   IN **7**   AQ **30**

Factor	Sten	Left Meaning	Standard Ten Score (STEN) 1 2 3 4 5 6 7 8 9 10	Right Meaning
A	10	RESERVED / Unengaging, Distant		SOCIABLE / Engaging, friendly
B	6	CONCRETE THINKING / Hands on learning		ABSTRACT THINKING / Independent learning
C	7	EASILY UPSET / Job should fit needs		MANAGES FRUSTRATION / Can adapt to job
E	10	SUBMISSIVE / More passive, humble		ASSERTIVE / Competitive, confident
F	8	SERIOUS / Sober, somber		ENTHUSIASTIC / Happy, lively, energetic
G	4	UNCONVENTIONAL / Ignores expectations		CONVENTIONAL / Follows rules
H	9	SOCIALLY RESTRAINED / Shy, avoids spotlight		SOCIALLY BOLD / Needs to impress others
I	7	TOUGH-MINDED / Realistic, no-nonsense		SENSITIVE / Susceptible to feelings
L	7	TRUSTING / Accepting, naïve		SUSPICIOUS / Skeptical, blaming
M	8	PRACTICAL / Focus on solutions		IMPRACTICAL / Focus on ideas
N	5	DIRECT WITH OTHERS / Self-disclosing, open		INDIRECT WITH OTHERS / Discreet, diplomatic, private
O	3	UNCONCERNED / Casual, untroubled		WORRYING / Fear of mistakes
Q1	10	RESISTS CHANGE / Prefers the familiar		OPEN TO CHANGE / Experimenting
Q2	2	WORKS IN GROUPS / Collaborative		WORKS ALONE / Independent, self-reliant
Q3	1	LESS ORDERLY / Can be undisciplined		MORE ORDERLY / Perfectionistic
Q4	9	PATIENT / Relaxed, calm		IMPATIENT / Tense, driven

GRAPH I — D I S C — 5 7 3 2 — PERSUADER

GRAPH II — D I S C — 7 6 3 1 — PERSUADER

Reasoning/Problem Solving

Raw Scores	Percentiles
L **54**	**82** %
Q **39**	**80** %
T **93**	**87** %

Norms Used - **MGR**

| CF **14/20** | **30** % |
| WG **36** | **85** % |

Norms Used - **MGR**

Global Factors

EX **10**

ER **7**

TM **1**

IN **10**

SC **2**

_____ Sten

Case Study 12.5 Intervention/Coaching[10]

---

[10] 16PF Profile adapted with permission from the Institute for Personality and Ability Testing, Inc. (2009). 16PF Fifth Edition Questionnaire Manual. Savoy, IL.

Case Study #6: Senior VP of Human Resources
Filling the Leadership Pipeline

Background

This is an individual with whom I have worked at an organizational level on several leadership projects and other executive leadership work as well. He was the vice president of human resources and at the time, he oversaw the legal and HR departments for a $600 million division of a $2 billion company in the automotive sector. He has since moved on to be senior vice president of human resources of a Fortune 500 company in the chemical sector. He continues to achieve higher levels of responsibility and successful roles. He is a great guy and tremendous leader. He would be on my list of people to recommend for a leadership team at any type of company. He has a strong sense of self without an overinflated ego. He is balanced in his personality and leadership ability and is constantly working on improving himself professionally.

Analysis

If you read back in chapter 11 and look at the eleven core traits that are identified in successful leaders, you will see he is gifted because he possesses all eleven traits we look for in successful leaders. His critical thinking skills and reasoning and problem-solving skills are well above average, with his perceptual reasoning (IQ) being near the superior range at 118 and his cognitive reasoning scores in the eightieth percentile. He has an MBA as well. His A7

(Warmth), Q2/6 (Self-Reliance), and I5 (Sensitivity) shows he has good people skills but is not reliant on the approval of others. He is intuitive and considerate of the needs of others and reads people and situations well. He has a high need to drive results and explore new ideas and ways of thinking as shown by his E7 (Assertive/Drive), H7 (Socially Bold), and Q1/9 (Open to Change).

He has the right amount of drive without running over people, as evidenced by his scores on E7 (Assertive/Drive), G6 (Rule Conscious), and Q3/8 (Organization). He has a strong professional presence: E7 (Assertive/Drive), F6 (Enthusiasm), and H7 (Socially Bold). If he had a fault, he was guilty of not delegating well enough, as shown in his G6 (Rule Conscious) and Q3/8 (Organization) but he made it a personal challenge to improve that competency. His DiSC confirms his struggles with delegating as he is a task-focused individual who looks for quantifiable results. His DiSC also confirms his competitive side, which shows his D (Dominance) being high on both graphs. This is a very strong profile of a very strong leader who continues to be successful wherever he goes.

The Executive Group
Profile Summary Graph (PSG)

Case Study #6 A. Sample

Filling the Leadership Pipeline Senior VP of Human Resources

PRIMARY PERSONALITY FACTORS   IM **22**   IN **0**   AQ **54**

Factor	Sten	Left Meaning	Standard Ten Score (STEN) 1 2 3 4 5 6 7 8 9 10	Right Meaning
A	7	RESERVED Unengaging, Distant	8	SOCIABLE Engaging, friendly
B	7	CONCRETE THINKING Hands on learning	8	ABSTRACT THINKING Independent learning
C	5	EASILY UPSET Job should fit needs	4	MANAGES FRUSTRATION Can adapt to job
E	7	SUBMISSIVE More passive, humble	8	ASSERTIVE Competitive, confident
F	6	SERIOUS Sober, somber	7	ENTHUSIASTIC Happy, lively, energetic
G	6	UNCONVENTIONAL Ignores expectations	7	CONVENTIONAL Follows rules
H	7	SOCIALLY RESTRAINED Shy, avoids spotlight	8	SOCIALLY BOLD Needs to impress others
I	5	TOUGH-MINDED Realistic, no-nonsense	4	SENSITIVE Susceptible to feelings
L	6	TRUSTING Accepting, naïve	7	SUSPICIOUS Skeptical, blaming
M	4	PRACTICAL Focus on solutions	3	IMPRACTICAL Focus on ideas
N	7	DIRECT WITH OTHERS Self-disclosing, open	8	INDIRECT WITH OTHERS Discreet, diplomatic, private
O	5	UNCONCERNED Casual, untroubled	4	WORRYING Fear of mistakes
Q1	9	RESISTS CHANGE Prefers the familiar	9	OPEN TO CHANGE Experimenting
Q2	6	WORKS IN GROUPS Collaborative	4	WORKS ALONE Independent, self-reliant
Q3	8	LESS ORDERLY Can be undisciplined	8	MORE ORDERLY Perfectionistic
Q4	3	PATIENT Relaxed, calm	2	IMPATIENT Tense, driven

GRAPH I	GRAPH II
D I S C	D I S C
5 6 2 4	6 3 1 6
PERSUADER	CREATIVE

Reasoning/Problem Solving **Global Factors**

Raw Scores Percentiles   EX __6__

L __49__ __70__ %   ER __5__

Q __39__ __80__ %   TM __4__

T __88__ __80__ %   IN __8__

Norms Used - **MGR**   SC __7__

CF __118__ __87__ %   __8__ Sten

WG ____ ____ %

Norms Used - ____

Case Study 12.6 Filling the Leadership Pipeline[11]

---

[11] 16PF Profile adapted with permission from the Institute for Personality and Ability Testing, Inc. (2009). 16PF Fifth Edition Questionnaire Manual. Savoy, IL.

Case Study #7: President
Succession Planning

Background

I saved the best for last and for good reason. I have used this individual's profile in my case studies for the last decade because it is a very solid profile of a very accomplished person. Not only does he have a tremendous track record everywhere he goes, he is a well-rounded, well-balanced leader and liked by all. I have had the privilege of working with this individual since 2001 and have watched him progress throughout his career. He has been successful in every role he has been in since I've been working with him.

When we began working together, he was head of logistics and part of the leadership team I was working with. When he was promoted to plant manager of that same company later on, he took me with him as his executive coach and to help him develop the new leadership team he had just inherited. After he left that position, he accepted an offer to be vice president of logistics for a worldwide automotive manufacturer and he again engaged me to help him build his staff. With his next career move he became vice president and general manager of a company with three steel plants and again he took me with him. After his first year, he had me conduct a 360 on him with his staff. Is it any wonder he has just been promoted to be president of that company? I have used this gentleman's profile for years because he possesses all the traits of a successful leader and has been successful everywhere he has been. He, too, possesses all eleven of the leadership traits I outlined in a previous chapter. His promotion to president speaks to the ability of using assessments to identify future talent as a viable means of supporting the talent management and leadership development initiatives. Here are his results:

Analysis

This individual shows strong progressive tendencies with a desire to push things forward and achieve strong outcomes, with his scores of E7 (Assertive/Drive), H7 (Socially Bold), and Q1/10 (Open to Change). He is intelligent, innovative, and thinks outside the box, with his scores of WG/40, B9 (Reasoning and Problem-Solving), I4 (Realistic), M5 (Practicality), and Q1/10 (Open to Change). He is well organized and very conscientious and has scores of G7 (Rule Conscious), and Q3/8 (Organization). He shows compassion and appreciation for others, as evidenced by A7 (Warmth), Q2/2 (Works in Groups/Group Dependent), and believes in the inherent goodness of others with his scores of L4 (Trusting) and I4 (Realistic).

His weakness is he is not quick to discipline and gives people the benefit of the doubt to the point where people often take advantage of him. He possesses good energy and drive, with scores of E7 (Assertive/Drive), F6 (Enthusiastic), H7 (Socially Bold); and his scores of Q1/10 (Open to Change), L4 (Trusting), and I4 (Realistic) suggest he is harder on himself than he is on others. Scores of E7 (Assertive/Drive), H7 (Socially Bold), and O3 (Unconcerned) reveal a strong confidence in himself without arrogance. He is creative, innovative, and progressive, with his scores of I4 (Realistic), M5 (Practicality), and Q1/10 (Open to Change). His track record is outstanding and, looking at his assessment results, you can see the strength in his personality. We continue to work together to help him build his leadership team currently, and he is a pleasure to work with.

The Executive Group
Profile Summary Graph (PSG)

Case Study #7   W. Sample

Succession Planning   President

PRIMARY PERSONALITY FACTORS   IM **12**   IN **0**   AQ **61**

Factor	Sten	Left Meaning	Standard Ten Score (STEN) 1 2 3 4 5 6 7 8 9 10	Right Meaning
A	7	RESERVED Unengaging, Distant		SOCIABLE Engaging, friendly
B	9	CONCRETE THINKING Hands on learning		ABSTRACT THINKING Independent learning
C	6	EASILY UPSET Job should fit needs		MANAGES FRUSTRATION Can adapt to job
E	7	SUBMISSIVE More passive, humble		ASSERTIVE Competitive, confident
F	6	SERIOUS Sober, somber		ENTHUSIASTIC Happy, lively, energetic
G	7	UNCONVENTIONAL Ignores expectations		CONVENTIONAL Follows rules
H	7	SOCIALLY RESTRAINED Shy, avoids spotlight		SOCIALLY BOLD Needs to impress others
I	4	TOUGH-MINDED Realistic, no-nonsense		SENSITIVE Susceptible to feelings
L	4	TRUSTING Accepting, naive		SUSPICIOUS Skeptical, blaming
M	5	PRACTICAL Focus on solutions		IMPRACTICAL Focus on ideas
N	5	DIRECT WITH OTHERS Self-disclosing, open		INDIRECT WITH OTHERS Discreet, diplomatic, private
O	3	UNCONCERNED Casual, untroubled		WORRYING Fear of mistakes
Q1	10	RESISTS CHANGE Prefers the familiar		OPEN TO CHANGE Experimenting
Q2	2	WORKS IN GROUPS Collaborative		WORKS ALONE Independent, self-reliant
Q3	8	LESS ORDERLY Can be undisciplined		MORE ORDERLY Perfectionistic
Q4	4	PATIENT Relaxed, calm		IMPATIENT Tense, driven

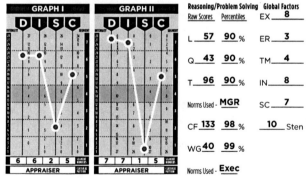

GRAPH I   D I S C   6 6 2 5   APPRAISER

GRAPH II   D I S C   7 7 1 5   APPRAISER

Reasoning/Problem Solving   Global Factors

Raw Scores	Percentiles		
L **57**	**90** %	EX	**8**
Q **43**	**90** %	ER	**3**
T **96**	**90** %	TM	**4**
Norms Used - **MGR**		IN	**8**
CF **133**	**98** %	SC	**7**
WG **40**	**99** %		**10** Sten
Norms Used - **Exec**			

Case Study 12.7 Succession Planning[12]

---

[12] 16PF Profile adapted with permission from the Institute for Personality and Ability Testing, Inc. (2009). 16PF Fifth Edition Questionnaire Manual. Savoy, IL.

Making Sense of the Case Studies

When evaluating assessment results, it is very rare that I give strong advice to not hire someone or not promote someone, as my intent is more about explaining how the various scores will help identify strengths, weaknesses, and a good job fit. As the case studies have shown, when the data is so compelling and suggests that a client is about to make a poor hire or promotion, or identify when someone is in the wrong position, I will strongly suggest that certain actions or measures be taken in the event the data reveals some overwhelming challenges. However, at the end of the day, it's not my call. It's only my advice based on twenty-five years of history using the assessments and the nearly 13,000 profiles I have evaluated to date.

The client has to make the call based on the information I provide from the results. The vast majority of the time the assessments I evaluate result in a discussion of the pros and cons of the profile, and how that integrates with the person's résumé and work history and job fit. The case studies presented here are some of the more extreme cases, but it is important to comprehend it only takes one really bad hire or a bad promotion to create a major problem.

My assessment and the process I developed is intended to help an organization understand an individual's strengths, weaknesses, and job fit with enough objective information to make a determination on to how to proceed. I have provided some of the more challenging profiles to show you how the data can enable you to avoid a bad hire or promotion but, more importantly, to show how a properly constructed set of assessments can further help build a strong leadership team and support the process of building a pipeline of strong talent. The case studies presented here support the notion that a properly designed battery of assessments provides compelling insight into someone's behavior, personality, job fit, and potential for job success. I think you will agree the information from these case studies is so compelling that you can see how a well-designed battery has strong predictive value when it comes to hiring, promoting, and developing people.

Additionally, a well-constructed assessment process will support the executive coaching and development process. If used properly, the results can avoid costly hiring and promotion mistakes. The unfortunate reality is that assessment results are rarely used to eliminate a candidate, whether it be for a new hire or a promotion. Hiring managers tend to resist the data, especially when it has the potential to knock out who they thought was their best candidate. I will explain why this often happens in a moment, but I frequently hear comments such as, "We don't want to use assessments to disqualify someone" or "We don't want to use assessments to eliminate someone." My first question is, "Why not?" and my second question is, "Do you really want to take the risk, as seen in the first five case studies, of hiring through old, traditional methods and wind up in a place you wish you were not?"

Another dynamic is that assessments are rarely given to someone internally who is being considered for promotion or for someone being placed in the high-potential pool. This is because the individual being considered is seen as a known commodity and it is assumed the person will succeed based on his current level of performance. After all, if someone is successful now, he will be successful in his next position. No one ever assumes the Peter Principle will occur but, in fact, success in one spot doesn't ensure success in a new role. Remember the great salesperson who became a sales manager and then failed. The previous examples I have provided throughout the book, including the promoted branch manager who almost inspired a union organizing, the executives from Coca-Cola, Mattel, Enron, American Apparel, and the case studies just presented here, dispel that notion. Assessments can and should be used to "screen" individuals to help choose the best of the best and the brightest, and "weed out" the weaker, less competent individuals. The data and case studies support the relevance of using assessments for selection, coaching, leadership development, filling the pipeline and, most importantly, supporting the succession planning process.

Not using assessments as one more data point to "weed out" lesser qualified candidates really is shortsighted. As you have seen from examples throughout this book, using assessments often prevent some poor hiring decisions. The case studies validate the use of assessments and show that you are prone to make bad hires, poor choices, and promote people to spots where they will be in over their heads by not listening to the data obtained from a quality assessment process.

One of the case studies presented is a classic example of what happens in an interview and that is our MBA, Big East engineering grad who is smart, charismatic, well-spoken, articulate, funny, and a big-picture thinker. He is going to get hired every time until his history catches up with him and someone begins to see the patterns in his résumé and work history. Here is another example of how a well-constructed battery of assessments can help reveal potential problems and gain deeper insight into a person's behavioral makeup.

Consider how many people never even get past the first step of a job application process. Individuals are constantly being eliminated for having poorly written résumés. Candidates are eliminated because of a poor phone interview, a poor personal interview, and are even eliminated for their lack of education. They are being eliminated after receiving poor references, failing a background check, or failing their drug and alcohol screening. Candidates are eliminated for all of the above reasons, but no one seems to want to eliminate a candidate who receives poor or negative assessment results. It seems implausible that corporations wouldn't value assessments as much as they do other aspects of the hiring process, including interviews and résumés. From a practical standpoint, companies should be relying on these assessments to make smarter hiring and promotion decisions.

The proper assessments, evaluated by a trained practitioner capable of interpreting the various instruments, will help reduce the subjective nature and personal biases common in the interview process. In addition, assessments provide a quantitative approach that supports and enhances the hiring process. The case studies presented here clearly point out not only the strengths these people possessed but their challenges as well, and how using the assessment data could have headed off a bad hire or a flawed promotion. I have seen over and over again that the assessment process is undervalued and underappreciated in its overall use in the talent management and leadership development process. What happens as a result is the misunderstanding of the relevance and value of the information is that decisions are made despite what the data tells us. On the other hand, using assessments to support a leadership development program provides a way to evaluate those people who are capable of filling the pipeline and understanding their strengths and weaknesses. In this way, you can then develop the proper coaching and development strategy to prepare them for success.

Assessments and the Evaluation Process

Assessments are typically given after the first interview. By this time the final candidates have already jumped through all the hoops and, by your own standards, you have eliminated all the other applicants and you are down to your last two or three suitable candidates. By this time the process has usually been dragged out and you just want to get the new person started and hope that you've chosen the right person. You interviewed them, the résumé looked impressive, the person had all the credentials, no red flags came back from the references, and during the interviews the candidate said all the right things. Everyone else you had interview her liked her as well! She *has* to be the right one. You tell yourself, "I couldn't have missed that much; I couldn't be that far off." After all, you say, "I am a good judge of character."

This scenario is no different when it comes to using assessments for internal promotions or for leadership development. However, in these cases, when the assessment results come back and they are less than favorable, or even strongly suggest that you would do better to find another candidate and it would not be in the best interest to hire or promote someone, you now say, "Oh, he must have not tested well," and then go on to find all the reasons to justify why the assessment does not count that much or you're not convinced that test results should carry that much weight. Your gut instinct and ego override the data. You are inclined to fight the data and keep thinking that the candidate has the right background, education, and skills so the data must be flawed. Hopefully, the case studies presented in this book show there is strong evidence to support the validity and reliability of the assessment process. Assessments can be used as a valuable piece to the puzzle when evaluating an individual for hire or for promotion. More importantly, the case studies show how a battery of assessments supports your entire talent management process and a world class leadership development program.

In Closing

The use of assessments in hiring, promoting, and developing a highly capable leadership team is an essential component of a world class leadership development program. By using them, you will fully understand the strengths and weaknesses of every individual and his true performance potential. When the time comes to identify the high potentials and fill the leadership pipeline you will be able to support the succession planning needs of the organization. Additionally, you will be able to create an in-depth development plan suited to the needs of everyone in the organization through the appropriate use of a well-designed battery of assessments.

Acknowledgements

There are so many people who have helped shaped my life, my business, and my career and, without whom, this book would never have been written. I want to thank the many clients who have allowed me to not only assist them in reaching their goals, but also to learn from them in ways that helped shape me professionally, as well as my business, and especially this book.

Many of those clients also have become close friends, and I want to thank them for volunteering to read my book and offer their thoughts: Tom Brown, Monica Della Valle, Paul Doerfler, Steve Hocker, Jim Kurtenbach, Peter Kyriacopoulos, Stewart McMillan, Joe Nelson, and Ron Rogers.

Deep appreciation goes to my mentors and coaches, Dr. Dave Watterson and Dr. Michael Karson, who have been instrumental in my knowledge of the assessment world. My mentors from years past, including Colonel E. B. Young, Major Norton, Captain Cross, Captain Shepard, and

Captain Mullin, taught me valuable lessons of leadership in my formidable years.

This book would never have happened without my staff: Sue Russell, my general manager and right hand since 1997. Thanks for sticking around through the many ups and downs. Jodie Wexelberg, my director of operations since 2006. Both of these ladies spent countless hours editing my writings over and over and over again. And, to Debbie Goodrich, my customer service/IT specialist, who gathered the information and guided the publishing of this book. Also, Carol Hazelgrove who oversees our marketing efforts and will be tasked with getting this book into the marketplace, as well as all those behind the scenes in getting a book published and to market. It takes a team to keep on winning, and I am blessed to have an awesome group of ladies to keep things running.

And to my many family members, Grandma Gingy, Mom, and Dad, I miss you so much and am grateful for all those valuable life lessons. My son Shane and his wife Sally, my grandchildren Aiden and Austin, and my son Nick and his wife Morgan, your love and support keeps me whole.

I hope this book gives you the guidance I received from others and makes a difference in your business and your lives.

About the Author

Rick Tiemann is founder and president of The Executive Group, a consulting firm specializing in organizational and business development, with an emphasis on leadership selection, development, and executive coaching. His expertise is helping organizations improve business performance outcomes. Since  1971, he has helped organizations design and implement human capital solutions to create business value, build high-performance teams, drive change, manage organizational effectiveness, and improve return on investment in people. He has led strategic planning initiatives, developed leadership teams, and developed sales strategies for improved sales outcomes.

He has worked from the C-suite to the plant floor with both national and international organizations, helping them to realize their potential. Clients that have engaged his services include Atlas Copco Compressors, Workiva, Printpack, Sysco Foods, Republic Services, Batesville Casket, and many more.

Rick is also a sought-after keynote speaker and presenter on topics ranging from leadership to selection to coaching and more. He has presented at many national conferences such as IHRIM, SHRM, and NAPL, as well as conducted workshops and presentations at the national and regional meetings for numerous multimillion-dollar corporations.

Rick lives in Valparaiso, Indiana, and has two sons, Shane and Nick, and two grandchildren.

To learn more about the products and services offered by The Executive Group, please visit, www.theeg.com.